"My dear brother Sam Rodriguez speaks clearly, writes convincingly and leads biblically. From hearing him talk before thousands to sitting over a meal talking man-to-man, I have come to know Sam as sincere in his life and rooted in his convictions. In our polarized world, Sam does not look for a middle ground but a higher ground, pointing others to Jesus."

Barry H. Corey, president, Biola University; author, *Make the Most of It: A Guide to Loving Your College Years*

"Samuel colorfully illustrates that when we infuse the 'anointed antibodies' of the Spirit against the infection of sin and failure, we become fully 'equipped to overcome, to defeat, to conquer and to triumph over the enemy.' A profound and timely book that is sure to help you persevere with power."

Matthew Crouch, president, Trinity Broadcasting Network

"*Persevere with Power* urges us to study the lives of the biblical heroes of the past so that we might better understand our present and walk with boldness into our future. If you are wondering how to move forward when it feels like life has come to a standstill, then this book is for you."

Dr. Tony Evans, senior pastor, Oak Cliff Bible Fellowship, Dallas, Texas; founder, The Urban Alternative; bestselling author

"At a time when the world is in crisis, *Persevere with Power* is the encouragement we all need. It is real and raw in its discussion of suffering, but it also inspires us to lift our eyes up to the mountains and remember where our help comes from."

Jentezen Franklin, senior pastor, Free Chapel; *New York Times* bestselling author

"Samuel Rodriguez shines a light on two Old Testament prophets God used and blessed because they were obedient to God's clarion call in the midst of a corrupt society. Readers will be captivated as they learn what God can do through those who faithfully take up the mantle of God's leading and persevere with power."

Franklin Graham, president and CEO, Billy Graham
Evangelistic Association and Samaritan's Purse

"In *Persevere with Power*, my good friend Rev. Rodriguez provides a blueprint for overcoming that should inspire us all. Although we find ourselves in challenging and desperate times, he proves through this book that we are not without hope! This is a must-read for everyone who needs a reminder that we are not fighting for victory; we are fighting *from* victory."

Pastor Nona Jones, head of faith-based partnerships, Facebook;
bestselling author, *Success from the Inside Out* and
From Social Media to Social Ministry

"Elijah and Elisha were God's answer to the evil leadership during the reign of Ahab and Jezebel. These two men were among the most influential prophets of Israel. Their supernatural interventions in national history—and the mighty miracles wrought by the power of God through them—serve as a reminder that the mantle placed upon them can be ours as well. In *Persevere with Power*, Pastor Samuel Rodriquez challenges his readers to pursue and take hold of the Holy Spirit's power that is given freely to each child of the living God. In this highly engaging and provocative book, you will learn how to tap into a deeper level of faith with courage and commitment, and persevere with the power of the Spirit."

Marcus D. Lamb, founder and president,
Daystar Television Network

"It's invigorating to read someone as passionate as Sammy Rodriguez on a subject he knows well. If you're feeling hopeless, exhausted or burdened, you'll come away from *Persevere with Power* freshly furnished to take on anything the enemy throws at you. When you're with Christ, you're on the winning side!"

Greg Laurie, senior pastor, Harvest Christian Fellowship

"The cancer journey I've been on, plus the COVID-19 lockdown, have been serious challenges to my momentum in service. Thank you, Sammy Rodriguez, for your fascinating insights into Elijah and Elisha, as well as the richness of your teaching, that have encouraged me to persevere with power. This is a book I will re-read and share with others."

Anne Graham Lotz, author, *Jesus in Me*

"My good friend Sammy Rodriquez tells us how we can rise up and be a light in these dark times. In *Persevere with Power*, Sammy challenges us to embrace the prophetic power available to us when we trust God. Through the stories of Elijah and Elisha—two men who stood against the evil leadership of their time—he inspires us to move forward in faith. Not only can you survive these times, but you can also receive a double portion of God's anointing! You have the power to overcome this world and leave a legacy for future generations."

Robert Morris, senior pastor, Gateway Church; bestselling author, *The Blessed Life*, *Beyond Blessed* and *Take the Day Off*

"*Persevere with Power* is a must-read. I love everything Pastor Samuel writes. This book will produce so much power inside of you. Life happens; it's messy and hard at times. But we have the power within us to persevere into greater! I'm changed because of the experiences that God has entrusted to me. This book will direct you into victory!"

Real Talk Kim, senior pastor, Limitless Church

"Powerful! A useful resource for every plowing season of your life. This is a book for those desiring the mantle and willing to push the plow."

Rosie Rivera, CEO, Jenni Rivera Enterprises;
author and evangelist

"My friend Sammy Rodriguez never fails to inspire. Throughout these pages, he encourages us to 'keep pushing our plows,' trusting that God is able to knock down any walls blocking our progress. The biblical examples of Elijah and Elisha woven throughout the book are powerful. May we all hunger for a double portion of the Spirit, power and anointing as Elisha desired—and like Elijah, may we seek to pass the mantle to the next generation."

James Robison, founder and president, LIFE Outreach
International, Fort Worth, Texas

"When we surrender our own plans and purposes to God's, miracles happen. I know that to be true because my life has been radically transformed by the power of Jesus Christ. No one is beyond redemption and restoration—that is the message at the heart of *Persevere with Power*."

Darryl Strawberry, evangelist; co-founder, Strawberry
Ministries; four-time World Series Champion;
New York Times bestselling author

PERSEVERE
WITH
POWER

PERSEVERE
WITH
POWER

WHAT HEAVEN STARTS,
HELL CANNOT STOP

SAMUEL RODRIGUEZ

Chosen
a division of Baker Publishing Group
Minneapolis, Minnesota

© 2021 by Samuel Rodriguez

Published by Chosen Books
11400 Hampshire Avenue South
Bloomington, Minnesota 55438
www.chosenbooks.com

Chosen Books is a division of
Baker Publishing Group, Grand Rapids, Michigan

Printed in the United States of America

ISBN 978-0-8007-6269-8

Library of Congress Cataloging-in-Publication Data
Names: Rodriguez, Samuel, 1969– author.
Title: Persevere with power : what heaven starts, hell cannot stop / Samuel Rodriguez.
Description: Minneapolis, Minnesota : Chosen Books, a division of Baker Publishing Group, [2021]
Identifiers: LCCN 2021023548 | ISBN 9780800762032 (cloth) | ISBN 9780800762049 (trade paper) | ISBN 9781493433582 (ebook)
Subjects: LCSH: Perseverance (Theology) | Power (Theology) | Elisha (Biblical prophet)
Classification: LCC BT768 .R63 2021 | DDC 232/.8—dc23
LC record available at https://lccn.loc.gov/2021023548

Cover design by Darren Welch Design

Baker Publishing Group publications use paper produced from sustainable forestry practices and post-consumer waste whenever possible.

21 22 23 24 25 26 27   7 6 5 4 3 2 1

I dedicate this book to my best friend,
basketball partner, pride and joy,
my personal "Elisha,"
my son, Nathan Samuel

Your father loves you beyond words.
Extremely proud of you.
Thank you for being a better version of me
by being who God made you to be.
Now go, change the world!

CONTENTS

FOREWORD

All of us love great stories. Whether we see them on the big screen or stream them on our televisions, we read them in novels or biographies, or we hear them as we sit around the family table, we anticipate plot twists, root for heroes and root against villains, and are thrilled by surprise endings. In the greatest adventure stories, a valiant hero always comes through even the most difficulty of challenges. My friend Pastor Sam is one of the greatest storytellers I know, and it's been a blessing for us to work together to produce hit Hollywood films like *Breakthrough*. With this book, *Persevere with Power*, I see all the elements of a compelling true story. The hero, though, isn't you and me; it's Jesus. He is the one who faces down venomous adversaries and rescues the helpless (us) from disaster. He is the protagonist in the drama, but you and I get to play important supporting roles.

Pastor Sam points us to the most gripping stories in the Bible. Page after page, he shows us how men and women of God faced roadblocks and breakthroughs, heartaches and heartbreaks. Sometimes they flinched, retreated or even failed, but they eventually held on to trust God to do what only He can do: deliver when we surrender. In His Word, God did not edit out the uncomfortable parts of the story—it is all there. And He did not try to hide the unvarnished realities of the struggle. It is there, woven into a narrative that sweeps us from creation to the fall into sin to the magnificent saga of redemption through Christ. And through Christ we are reminded that our story has a powerful ending!

This book peels off any blinders we might use because we are afraid of the truth. When we see things as they are, we notice the layers of reality—physical, relational, cultural, emotional and spiritual. We are in a fight, but it is not only against things we can see. Our real battle is against things we can't see. We see personal tragedies, family calamities, cultural threats, economic setbacks and political division, but behind all these are spiritual forces of darkness that try to demoralize us and shatter our faith.

In each chapter, Pastor Sam shows how we can trust the Savior's sacrifice and the Spirit's power to be overcomers. In Paul's greatest theological dissertation, the letter to the Romans, he catalogs a list of difficulties believers face—tribulation, distress, famine, danger or sword—but none of these have the last word. He boldly proclaims, "No, in all these things we are more than conquerors through him who loved us" (Romans 8:37). That is what this book is about: conquering through Christ.

Persevere with Power is both inspirational and practical. In each chapter, Pastor Sam provides clear points of application so we can actually incorporate spiritual truth into our hearts and our choices. And he goes further: At the end of each chapter, we find penetrating questions designed to expose our needs and target the Spirit's work. Pastor Sam then ends each chapter with a prayer that captures the heart of faith and our request for God to work miracles.

Do you see your life as a compelling story, with plot twists and the ultimate hero? Great stories always include steep obstacles and fierce adversaries. I'm sure you have them—all of us do. Pastor Sam asks us to invite Jesus into the middle of our mess, to trust that God will show us the way over the obstacles and give us the strength to face our enemies. When Jesus is in the center of it all, we experience the beautiful blend of God's power, His love and our fulfillment.

Isn't that the kind of story you want your life to tell?

DeVon Franklin, producer, author and friend

INTRODUCTION

The Bible is not the book of perfect people. The Bible is not a historical categorization of pristine, unblemished, stainless saints. No! Without a doubt, from Genesis to Revelation, the Bible is a book of overcomers. Just look at some of the most famous of the faithful and what they overcame:

Abraham overcame the deceit of others as well as his own lies.

Joseph overcame the pit and the betrayal of his own brothers.

Moses overcame Pharaoh, his temper and his past.

Joshua overcame the Amalekites, the disobedience of his troops and his fear of being alone when his mentor died.

Gideon overcame the threshing floor and his insecurities.

Samson overcame his pride, his lack of respect for the anointing and Delilah's deception.

David overcame a bear, a lion, a giant, Saul's spear and his own moral turpitude.

Elijah overcame Jezebel.

Elisha overcame famine and siege.

Esther overcame the haters.

Daniel overcame the lions.

The Hebrew boys overcame the furnace.

Job overcame the loss of all he had.

Peter overcame the cursing of his blessing.

Paul overcame the shipwreck and the snake.

And Jesus, the Son of God and our wondrous Savior, Jesus
overcame darkness, death and defeat. Jesus overcame
everything!

No matter what you are facing right now, your battle might not
be over but it has already been won. God will never give up on you
and will instead anoint you with strength to help you overcome
the powers of darkness that are trying to defeat you.

In this book we will take a hard look at what it means to persevere with power—to walk in the confidence that hell cannot
stop the prophetic anointing that God has placed on your life.
Put another way, you will learn how to keep your hand to the
plow spiritually. If you are willing to do this, to push your plow
spiritually, then you can know that God's mantle of anointing and
power is waiting for you. And when God's mantle rests on your
shoulders, then nothing or no one can stop you! Because—as we
will learn from the struggles of two of the greatest prophets in
world history—when the Elijahs speak up, the Jezebels cannot
win. When the Elishas stand up, the Ahabs cannot endure. When
you and I as God's people pray down fire, it makes no difference
how soaking wet the altar is; Baal cannot win.

No matter how bleak your circumstances, God's power in you
will prevail. Nothing is finished until God declares it finished. So
let me declare something prophetically: When future believers

write about our generation, our time in history, they will not say, "This was the generation of Jezebel, Ahab or Baal." They will say, "This was the generation when the blood-washed, Holy Spirit-filled, devil-rebuking, demon-binding, grace-filled, righteous-living Elijahs and Elishas stood up!"

Porque lo que es de Dios siempre gana!

Did you catch the meaning in those words? We will be remembered as overcomers *because those who are of God always win!*

The most powerful spirit on the planet today is not the spirit of consumerism or greed, and it is not the spirit of influence and affluence. The most powerful spirit on the planet *was* and *still is*, back then and right now, and always will be *the Holy Spirit of almighty God.*

When you have the Spirit of God dwelling in you, then you never have to fear again the times you live in. As a follower of Jesus who has accepted the free gift of salvation through His sacrifice on the cross, you are assured that "you have received the Holy Spirit, and he lives within you" (1 John 2:27 NLT). You may face trials and tribulations, you may endure storms and setbacks, but you will never be defeated permanently. You might experience discomfort, distress or debilitation, but your joy and peace will not cease.

If you have that Spirit, then you will speak as if you have Him.

If you have that Spirit, then you will praise as if you have Him.

If you have that Spirit, then you will worship as if you have Him.

If you have that Spirit, then you will fight as if you have Him.

If you have that Spirit, then you will pray as if you have Him.

If you have that Spirit, then you will rebuke the devil as if you have Him.

If you have that Spirit, then everything about your life is in Him and through Him and by His power.

Here is the truth about overcoming the struggles we face.

When you are washed by the blood of the Lamb . . .

When you are forgiven through Christ's death on the cross . . .

When you are filled with the Holy Spirit . . .

When Jesus is Lord and Savior of your life . . .

Then you are *not* who you used to be!

You are not an eternal victim.

You are not the devil's punching bag.

You are not cursed.

You are not defeated.

When you have the mantle of God resting on your shoulders, you no longer depend on your own abilities. You no longer face your own limitations or the caveats and qualifications others try to impose on you. You no longer rely on your own strength because you understand that the unlimited, infinite and eternal power of the great I AM is inside you. And you are never the same.

Come with me to learn how in Christ, by Christ, through Christ and for Christ, you can overcome. You can *persevere with power*!

1

Prophetic Power
for Pathetic Times

When you live in the power of the Holy Spirit, you can walk through any circumstance—no matter how challenging!

Sam, I'm taking Yvonne to the emergency room—she has a fever and she's . . . she's gasping for breath." My wife's voice choked with emotion then as only a mother's can for her child. *"I think she has the virus."*

With that one short sentence, my faith was suddenly tossed into a Category 5 hurricane. Our oldest daughter, Yvonne, a mother of two young children herself, my grandchildren, had been feeling poorly for several days. My wife, Eva, who trained as a combat nurse during her military career, had been taking care of Yvonne as well as her little ones. If Eva thought our daughter needed emergency care for the potential effects of COVID-19, then I knew she had based her opinion on painful reality.

My precious daughter did indeed test positive for the deadly virus and was admitted to the hospital. I have never felt more helpless and powerless in my life than when I saw her lying in a hospital bed on the screen of my phone—I could not even visit her in person because of the preventative measures taken by the hospital. Our church began praying around the clock for her recovery, along with the restoration of health for everyone suffering the life-threatening impact of that unprecedented viral assault on humanity.

I continued ministering and serving as best I could, if only to pour my energy into something constructive rather than ruminating on the dark thoughts gathering at the edge of my mind like storm clouds. To combat the worst-case scenarios darting through my mind, I took every thought captive and clung to the promises of God in His Word. I know He is inherently good and loves His children. I know that by the power of His Spirit and the blood of His Son, Jesus Christ, I can do all things.

Then the enemy would tempt me with graphic reminders of the toll the coronavirus was taking. The way it defied analysis and seemed to behave erratically in individual cases. I wanted to believe that my daughter's healthy body could sustain the attack, but then I would see cases of other young adults who never recovered. I wanted to believe that her immune system would aggressively develop antibodies, the invisible protein cells generated in her plasma to counter the invading virus, but then I would wonder, *What if, for some reason, her body cannot fight back?*

I wanted to believe that she could not possibly die, that God loved her—and me and my wife—too much to allow such a devastating loss. But then I would think of other men and women of God whom I knew, in our church and in my pastoral network of relationships, who endured the loss of loved ones, including their children. I worked hard to sustain my faith and remain strong for Eva and for Yvonne and her own young family.

When I was alone, though, the emotions would bubble from inside my heart until I could no longer contain my tears. I remember driving myself home from my office. I would be cruising down the highway and suddenly realize my vision had grown blurry, almost as if it were raining on my windshield. The tears spilled out so hard and fast a couple times that I had to pull over, sobbing and crying out to God, begging Him to obliterate the virus from my daughter's body, praying His Spirit would give us all the supernatural peace that is beyond earthly understanding.

Then the unthinkable happened: Yvonne was moved to the hospital's Intensive Care Unit because her lungs were losing capacity. She was put on a ventilator and given stronger steroids. Her doctors told us that her body was not generating adequate antibodies to fight the virus.

Though I had felt powerless in the days leading up to that moment, nothing was like the impact of those words. I truly did not know how I could go forward.

I felt as if I had wandered into a deep, dark cave with no way out.

Afraid of the Dark

During those dark days when we walked with Yvonne through the battle for her life, I knew, as I mentioned, that I was not the only one suffering. The shadow of the pandemic spread across our families, our neighborhoods, our workplaces, our communities and our churches. Loved ones lost, businesses shuttered, careers stalled, events postponed, homes locked, hopes and dreams suspended—for the rest of their lives millions and millions of people will grapple with seismic shifts, struggling to reorient themselves to a different world.

Even people blessed enough at the time to have remained healthy, maintained their employment and shepherded their families through the valley of the shadow of death still tell me to this day how they struggle. Some feel traumatized by the possibility of the unimaginable once again upending their lives. Others wrestle with chronic, ambiguous grief because they saw so much suffering around them.

No matter the age and stage of life in which we find ourselves, darkness inevitably descends. When we are in it, everything suddenly seems unfamiliar and uncertain. We grope along, sometimes afraid to ignite even a flicker of hope because something else might happen to quench that small spark of light. We try to trust God and rely on Him to lead us forward and guide our steps. We try to exercise faith and not allow fear, anger, sorrow and doubt to consume us.

And if we are able to emerge from darkness, we still struggle. When the darkness has lifted, many of us resist acknowledging that it even exists. It is simply too painful and stirs up too many overwhelming memories of the past. Why consider something unpleasant, we reason, when our lives are going well enough and everything colors within the lines of our expectations? Once we have experienced the fragility of life and the way almost every aspect of our world can change, literally overnight, then we have a whole new basement for the worst-case scenarios haunting our imaginations.

Either way, regardless of our circumstances, we often end up afraid of the dark, afraid to face what might be there.

When the Worst Happens

As much as I wish I were immune to trials and tribulations, I am right there with you, just like everyone trying to keep the faith and take each day as it comes. While in many ways my faith is stronger than ever, I also know what it feels like to have the unfathomable become reality. All it takes, really, is one moment, one text, one email, one phone call.

In fact, if you are like me, you are probably tempted to feel overwhelmed by the times in which we live. Political division and social distancing; civil unrest and systemic racism; bankrupt morality and cultural promiscuity. We could each make our own lengthy lists of the triggers of tension in our lives right now.

The toll of such ongoing, unrelenting stress leads to chronic anxiety, depression and fatigue. Whom can we trust for truth in the swirl of so much sensationalism, social media spin and fake news? We truly live in unprecedented times, and the cumulative weight of so much pain, grief, anger and negativity can shatter our lives and derail our relationship with God—if we let it.

But we always have a choice, and our choice right now is clear: We can give in to our emotions amidst overwhelming, tumultuous circumstances, or we can live by faith through the power of the living God. Despite my struggles and moments of doubt, I believe the only choice forward is by faith. I believe the only source of truth we can trust—above and beyond any other—is God's Word. And when I look to Scripture to light the path in this present darkness, I turn to the example I find there in two heroes of the faith.

You see, the genesis of this book was my search for biblical precedent for hope amidst the darkest of times. I wanted to see if Scripture provided an example that can serve as a template for these distressing days in which we are living. And if so, I wanted to see evidence of God's promise to respond to His people with an outpouring of prophetic power. Many questions formed in my mind: How did those people keep their hope alive, their faith intact when all was darkness around them? What understanding did they have that gave them strength and brought them through their valleys? Is it available to us in equal measure? How do we access it?

While numerous possibilities came to mind, I felt led to the story of the relationship between two Old Testament prophets, Elijah and his successor, Elisha. I have always been inspired by the diligence, dedication and devotion displayed in their lives during one of Israel's darkest historical periods. They lived during one of the most corrupt, violent, immoral times ever and yet remained faithful to God and experienced His faithfulness, power and provision in the face of impossible odds.

A Match Made in Hell

Look briefly at the world in which Elijah and Elisha lived. By the time Ahab claimed the throne, more than a century had passed since King David had reigned over Israel, and the nation of God's chosen people had split into two weaker fragments. David's descendants continued to rule the Southern Kingdom of Judah, while the Northern Kingdom of Israel endured a plague of toxic kings one after another, culminating in the person of Ahab. Amidst a list of notorious, nefarious, no-good leaders, it is telling that Ahab is introduced as the worst yet: "Ahab son of Omri did more evil in the eyes of the LORD than any of those before him" (1 Kings 16:30).

This is the first instance when Ahab's name appears in Scripture—talk about first impressions! Right away we are told he was more rebellious, degenerate and evil than any of his predecessors. And he definitely lived up to this reputation in his selection of a wife: "He not only considered it trivial to commit the sins of Jeroboam son of Nebat, but he also married Jezebel daughter of Ethbaal king of the Sidonians, and began to serve Baal and worship him" (1 Kings 16:31).

Basically, Ahab chose his queen for advantageous political reasons, but given the fact that her father is cited by name, a name identifying him as a priest of the false god Baal, it is clear she was a match made in hell for the equally idolatrous Ahab. She came from a household and culture that worshiped idols and listened to false prophets. Jezebel, as it turns out, may have been even worse than her wicked husband.

She hated the prophets.

She persecuted the preachers.

She rejected the truth.

In fact, as you may recall, after Elijah's display of God's power in a showdown on Mount Carmel against hundreds of Jezebel's false prophets, which led to their deaths, Jezebel in turn threatened the Lord's chosen prophet with death.

Consequently, Elijah became afraid and ran away. As we will see, he had to push a metaphorical plow before he could resume his ministry with the mantle God had placed on him.

Elijah was a man with a mantle.

A man with a message.

A man with a mission.

Then, after persevering through his own trials precipitated by Ahab and Jezebel, Elijah went in search of the person God had anointed to join him on his mission, a man named Elisha.

The essence of their message emerges vividly in the first meeting between our two prophets:

> So Elijah went and found Elisha son of Shaphat plowing a field. There were twelve teams of oxen in the field, and Elisha was plowing with the twelfth team. Elijah went over to him and threw his cloak across his shoulders and then walked away.
>
> 1 Kings 19:19 NLT

Look at that key Scripture again: When the older prophet arrived to see the younger man pushing a plow, breaking ground and sowing seeds in faithful service to God, Elijah placed his mantle upon Elisha and walked away.

That mantle changed Elisha's life and shifted the trajectory of a nation.

One that would subsequently embody the notion of a greater portion.

Elisha's plow prepared him to wear God's mantle and wield the power and responsibility that came with it. The same cause-and-effect sequence of spiritual growth and unlimited holy power continues to operate today. When we carry out faithfully the roles and responsibilities, the duties and directives that God assigns to us, then He gives us more—more power, more provision, more passion—to meet the next challenges we are called to face.

No matter how dark our night, God's morning always comes.

No matter how downcast we may feel, God's presence is always with us.

No matter how desperate our circumstances, God's power always prevails.

Hard times may leave us in darkness, but they can never separate us from the Light.

This Present Darkness

I am convinced and convicted that 1 Kings 18 and 19 speak to this very hour in which we live. Our world, spiritually speaking, bears a remarkable resemblance to the time of King Ahab and Queen Jezebel, leaders of Israel who not only served as antagonists for Elijah and Elisha but also represent the antithesis of everything holy. Simply put, Ahab was a horrible king and a *mucho malo hombre*. And his wife was even worse—evil on steroids!

Spiritually speaking, Ahab represents forces that tempt and prompt us to sacrifice truth on the altar of expediency. These forces try to tell us what to believe and how to act, coercing us into conforming to their own idolatrous agendas rather than obeying the Word of God. They are the political leaders doing whatever is expedient for their own power and profit, pretending to care about their constituents but intent on exploiting them. They are the social media celebrities and style icons, seducing followers to imitate them without any limits to their language, behavior and morality. They are the corporate executives and media moguls driven by greed and worshiping mammon rather than the truth of the living God.

Concurrent with the obliteration of biblical truth in our culture, Jezebel represents the manipulative, sexually coercive, perverse, corrupt spirit determined to murder goodness, poison innocence and silence prophetic voices. Modern Jezebels want to construct counterfeit temples and legitimize bogus institutions that will marginalize noble, God-honoring oracles of righteousness and justice. They are the entertainers offering their self-aggrandizing authority and the advertisers selling self-delusion and vanity. They construct their Asherah poles, or some other dispenser of noxious noise, and try to drown out the cries of the persecuted, the impoverished, the wounded.

In the 21st century, in the United States and around the world, we cannot deny that the spirit of Jezebel is alive and well, thriving voraciously in our midst where once it was forced to hide. Rather than covert seductions and individual corruption, now we see leaders and entire organizations persecuting, prosecuting and attempting to silence the children of the cross. The spirit of Ahab is alive and well, stealing love, killing joy and destroying peace. The spirit of Baal is alive and kicking, demanding that truth and children in and out of the womb be sacrificed on the altar of self-defined autonomy.

The word that I use most often to describe such dark and desperate times is *pathetic*. I like the way its two primary definitions both apply: It means "something wretched" as well as "something useless and contemptible." Derived from the Greek word *pathos*, meaning "suffering" or "feeling," *pathetic* most likely entered the English language in the sixteenth century and referred to that which evoked pity bordering on sympathy. While *sympathy* allows us to acknowledge loss or tragedy in the lives of others and feel the weight of their grief, *pity*, on the other hand, carries the sense of recognizing pain without valuing it. Yes, pity sometimes is used synonymously with sympathy or mercy, but usually *pity* harkens back to its pathetic roots.

But here is the Good News, the truth at the heart of the Gospel: *Pathetic times last for a while but God's prophetic power always triumphs!*

Anointed Antibodies

I saw this truth illustrated firsthand in my daughter's recovery. When Yvonne's body failed to produce enough antibodies on its own to combat the viral infection, her doctors realized that her best chance of recovery was using power appropriated from another source. In this case, such treatment meant injecting into her body plasma and antibodies from someone else, someone with her same blood type who had already contracted the coronavirus and recovered. Her doctors hoped her body would circulate the new antibodies and perhaps stimulate the creation of more of her own, offering a kind of dual antibody attack on the virus.

There was risk involved, of course, but it was the best possible course of treatment available, the one with the greatest chance of succeeding. After two weeks in the hospital, with much of that time spent in the ICU, Yvonne began to recover. Her body's systems began to resume their normal functioning, especially her respiratory system, and her symptoms began to fade. Injecting antibodies from another patient who had already recovered proved successful. Her body now had the antibodies it needed. Within hours of this treatment, she began making a full recovery and was soon discharged from the hospital.

After I wept for joy and prayed with praise and thanksgiving to the Great Physician, I reflected upon the symbolism of my daughter's treatment. The more I considered everything I had learned about the way viruses attack the human body, the more similarities I saw in the assault of evil on our spiritual health. It presented a unique illustration, metaphorically and spiritually speaking, of what takes place when a spiritual virus gets an inroad into our souls, our hearts, our faith, our families and our communities. A virus is a microscopic infectious entity, a foreign substance that seeks living cells for the purpose of replicating itself. In other words, it does not belong where it lands, just as darkness does not belong in our souls. Evil always seeks to kill and destroy. The enemy, like a virus, persists in tempting us with defeat until we grow weaker and more vulnerable. At the very worst, we give up and allow sin into our lives, which affects every area, every decision, every relationship.

There is an antidote, however. Hope—the unwavering belief in the goodness of God—counterattacks darkness like powerful antibodies. Antibodies recognize foreign substances like bacteria and viruses, and neutralize them. They also stay on guard in order to provide protection against future exposures.

In other words, because you survived, now you are stronger.

If you are stronger, then you will defeat the darkness when it tries to infect you again.

Do you see the spiritual connection?

Think of the many people in Scripture who were infected by evil, fell into sin and were swept away. This is where the story of Elisha and Elijah is crucial to understand if we are going to survive individually and as God's people. Darkness, if left unchecked, will pull us from the forward march of faith and throw us into the grip of fear and defeat.

But every time we stand and win the battle against darkness, then we are equipped to overcome, to defeat, to conquer and to triumph over that enemy the next time it tries to infect our lives.

What an extraordinary picture of the way God empowers us with His Spirit to defeat darkness! Never doubt that God has anointed you with spiritual antibodies to overcome the virus of pathetic times.

The Choices

If Elijah and Elisha had given up and stopped trusting God, then they would have missed out. If they had not persevered with pushing their respective plows, one metaphorical and the other literal, then they would have missed the mantle of blessing God had for them. The Lord would still have defeated His enemies and provided prophetic power to overcome such pathetic times, but He would have used someone else.

You and I can be part of what God is doing, or we can sink into the cultural muck trying to pull us under. We can thrash and splash as the relentless currents of unexpected circumstances overwhelm us, or we can grab the lifeline of prophetic power

God extends to those who trust Him. We cannot control all that happens to us and around us, but we always have a choice about how we respond.

We can choose to keep plowing, faithfully and obediently, even when we are tired, afraid, anxious and sad, trusting God to know when we are ready to wear His mantle and move on. Or we can abandon our plows and lose ourselves in the wilderness of hedonism and humanism surrounding us. We can refuse to keep going and trusting God and instead listen to the voices of false prophets, idolaters and other wolves in sheep's clothing.

And even when we fail, we can rejoice that God is faithful! Despite the repeated disobedience and frequent idolatry of the people of Israel, God did not abandon them but sent prophets, including Elijah and Elisha, with His message of repentance and His power to conquer adversity. Ahab and Jezebel blatantly worshiped pagan gods and practiced rituals and customs abhorrent to the Lord of lords. We are told they were the worst of the worst, the bottom of the barrel, the lowest of lows despite their royal status at the top of their social and cultural hierarchy. They thought they had won and had proved that the God of their ancestors was no longer relevant, reliable or relatable.

Unbeknown to Ahab and Jezebel, however, they had simply created an opportunity for God to reveal His prophetic power through His people. What they intended for their own glory, greed and pleasure, God used as a showcase to spotlight His character, His love and His mercy.

Do not be distracted, my friend, by the ever-changing demands on your life.

Do not leave your plow behind because you are too weary, too afraid or too unsure.

Do not give up hope when God is preparing you for your breakthrough.

Do not despair when sin tries to infect your life.

Pathetic times are no match for the limitless prophetic power of the living God!

Choosing Prophetic over Pathetic

While you and I have never witnessed anything like the challenges of recent times, God has. He exists outside of chronological time as we know it, and His omniscience knows all that can be known, far beyond what mortal minds can comprehend or human senses can engage. God is not surprised by anything that is happening right now—not in your life, your family, your neighborhood, your community, your workplace, your church, your city, your county, your state, your nation or your world.

Whether you realize it or not, God has prepared you for times such as these. He has already anointed you with antibodies for the virus of a sinful world that is trying to infect your life. When the world turns upside down, God is the same as He has always been. When the light around you grows dim, the Light inside you shines brighter. James assures us that "every good and perfect gift is from above, coming down from the Father of the heavenly lights, who does not change like shifting shadows" (James 1:17). God sees what you are facing and He will meet you in the midst of your struggles.

He might not show you the end of your story just yet, and He might not provide what you want when you want it. You might have to take it a step at a time, a day at a time rather than be magically transported into a life free of pain or discomfort. Nonetheless, God is with you and will not leave you defenseless in the face of evil. If you are willing to let go of how you want your life to be, then God can begin showing you what your life *can* become—a trophy of His grace, a testimony of His power, a spiritual mirror of His glory.

Why do I know this? Not because God healed my daughter, not because of the abundance of blessings He has faithfully bestowed on me and my family throughout my life, and not because of how I feel yesterday, today or tomorrow. I know God cares about you and wants to drape your soul with His mantle of protection, power and provision because this is who He is and has always been and will always be. This is the great I AM who loves us relentlessly despite our failures, flaws and fluctuations. This is who God is in the Old Testament, who He is in the New Testament, and who He is in this present moment.

Push Your Plow, Meet Your Mantle

At the end of each chapter, you will find a few questions to help you reflect on my message and apply it to your own life. There is no obligation; this is not homework. And you do not have to write down your responses, but you might be surprised to discover how helpful it can be to keep a record of how God speaks to you through these pages.

Whether you record your answers or not, after you have spent a few moments thinking about these questions, I encourage you to go to the Lord in prayer and share with Him what is going on in your heart. To help ignite your conversation with God, to help spark your communication with Him, I have provided a short prayer for you. No matter what you are facing, remember that He is your heavenly Father, your Creator and the Lover of your soul.

The plow you are pushing today is preparing you for the mantle you will wear tomorrow.

1. What are the hardest things you are facing right now? What burdens are you carrying that weigh the most on your soul? How have you handled their pressure so far?

2. What examples do you see in the world around you that parallel the pathetic times during which Ahab and Jezebel ruled? What trends, issues and conflicts concern you the most in your community right now? What frightens you most about them? What impact are they having on your life? On the lives of those you love?

3. How have you seen God meet you in the midst of your struggles lately? What do you need from Him most right now?

Dear God, I need You now more than ever! I want to trust You and walk by faith each day, every day, but it is hard when everything feels overwhelming. I know You are present in my life and in my heart even when my feelings cloud my spiritual senses. Hear my prayer, Lord, and the cries of my heart as I surrender all the grief, anger, fear, anxiety and depression lingering inside me. Fill me with Your Spirit so that I may be renewed, refreshed and recharged. Empower me to push the plow placed before me so that I can be ready when the time comes to wear the mantle You want to give me. Amen.

2

Pushing the Plow

Pushing your plow prepares you for wearing the mantle God has for you. Never confuse what you are going *through* with where you are going *to*!

Some stories inspire us more than others.

Now that I participate in the production of faith-based films and media, I have started analyzing what makes certain characters, events and stories more powerful, hopeful and life-giving than others. Curiously enough, I have also been inundated with story ideas from a multitude of sources.

Usually when people I meet find out I am a pastor, they get a certain look, an expression that conveys polite reservation and resistance to any evangelizing that they anticipate might take place. When I mention that I am a die-hard sci-fi fan, movie buff and aspiring producer involved with movies such as *Breakthrough*, however, suddenly everyone wants to be my friend and pitch his or her movie idea! I am still not exactly sure why some stories captivate me more than others, but like millions of viewers,

I want to care about characters with whom I identify while being challenged and inspired to grow stronger in my Christian faith.

Which explains why I was drawn to the story of Richard Montañez. In many ways, Mr. Montañez started life like so many hard-working people I know. A little older than I am, he grew up in a poor farming community east of Los Angeles. He and a dozen members of his family lived in a one-room cinder-block house within a migrant labor camp, picking grapes and working seasonal jobs. Much later, he summed up his childhood to a reporter for the *Washington Post* by declaring, "I have a PhD of being poor, hungry and determined."[1]

Montañez dropped out of school in the fourth grade to help provide for his family, doing odd jobs, washing cars and working in a slaughterhouse. When he was eighteen, he heard through the community grapevine that the Frito-Lay plant in Rancho Cucamonga was hiring. Barely able to read and write, he needed help to complete his application, provided by the young woman who later became his wife. Frito-Lay hired him as a janitor at $4 an hour, and, instead of being disappointed, Montañez took his grandfather's work ethic to heart. "Make sure that floor shines," his *abuelo* told him. "And let them know that a Montañez mopped it."[2]

One day at work, one of the machines broke down on the Cheetos assembly line, resulting in a plain batch without the signature cheese powder dust. Never one to waste free food, Montañez took

1. Kathleen Elkins, "How a Janitor Invented Flamin' Hot Cheetos and Became an Exec at PepsiCo," *CNBC*, June 29, 2018, https://www.cnbc.com/2018/03/27/a-janitor-invented -flamin-hot-cheetos-and-became-a-pepsico-exec.html; see also https://www.washingtonpost .com/news/morning-mix/wp/2018/02/23/the-flamin-hot-cheetos-movie-how-a-frito-lay -janitor-created-one-of-americas-most-popular-snacks/.

2. Andrew Whalen, "The True Story of the Flamin' Hot Cheetos Inventor Richard Montañez," *Newsweek*, August 27, 2019, https://www.newsweek.com/flamin-hot-cheeto -movie-true-story-creator-richard-montanez-1456377.

some plain Cheetos home and decided to try out a different, spicy flavor mixture. He loved the grilled corn drizzled with lime juice and chili powder sold by street vendors in his neighborhood and was inspired to create a similar flavored coating for his accidental Cheetos.

Friends and family loved his new creation so much that Montañez decided he would pitch it to Roger Enrico, then CEO of PepsiCo, the corporate parent of Frito-Lay. Simultaneously naïve and bold, Montañez did not realize that employees, especially a janitor at a factory, should not call up the top leader with new ideas. Enrico's assistant, however, put Montañez's call through to her boss, who agreed to a taste-testing presentation in two weeks.

Encouraged by the enormous opportunity presented to him, Montañez headed to his local library and, with help from bilingual family and friends, scrambled to understand marketing, branding and the snack retail industry. He became a quick study and focused on every detail of his presentation, including original packaging with clever brand graphics. And that is how Flamin' Hot Cheetos, one of the world's most popular and bestselling snacks ever, was born.

Needless to say, Montañez leaped his way up the corporate ladder after such an original, wildly successful idea. He became an executive for PepsiCo until he decided to consult and motivate other companies to promote diversity and creativity at every level. And I am proud to say that I am part of a group of producers making a movie for Fox Searchlight Pictures about this innovator's extraordinary journey.

Many will likely consider his story a rags-to-riches tale illustrating the promise of the American Dream. But others, myself included, will be reminded that you must be willing to push the plow before you can wear the mantle.

Plowing in 3-D

Stories like Richard Montañez's journey provide hope that dreams are worth pursuing no matter how out of reach they may initially appear. I am convinced it is why people love to see an underdog overcome impossible odds and defeat a superior adversary. Whether it is David slaying the boasts of an arrogant Goliath, my Pittsburgh Pirates coming back to win Game 7 of the 1971 World Series against the Baltimore Orioles, or the 1980 U.S. Men's Olympic hockey team surprisingly capturing the gold, we root for those who refuse to give up. Cinderella triumphed over the schemes of her stepmother and stepsisters, just as Cinderella sports teams transform pumpkin plays into championship trophies.

Arguably, some underdogs seem to win by sheer luck. Most, however, win by doing the hard work required to put them into position to make the right move at the right time. They expend the hours, days, weeks and years necessary to make every free throw, hit every pitch, catch every pass and sink every putt. Even if they do not always believe in themselves and feel inferior to their competitors, they still believe in hard work.

Such commitment and dedication is not exclusive to athletes, of course. The same devotion to fundamentals can be seen in virtually every field. The vast majority of people who achieve a consistent level of success have put in the time, energy, focus, resources and practice required to maximize their abilities and to actualize their passion for their profession. Computer engineers, district attorneys, neurosurgeons and building contractors do not just decide one day to create software, win criminal cases, save lives or construct homes. Instead, years prior to reaching a level of competency, let alone mastery, they did the hard work of starting and then sustaining.

In his bestselling book *Outliers*, popular author and social observer Malcolm Gladwell shares his research into what makes some people more successful than others. All variables being equal, which he acknowledges is rarely, if ever, the case, the difference between good and great, between elite performers in their fields and those who are merely competent, is relentless practice. The people who achieve the most are the ones who put in the most time.

Gladwell affirms that on average most superstars—whether in medicine, music, sports, technology, arts or entertainment—invest at least ten thousand hours of dedicated practice in order to achieve the stellar results for which they are known. "The closer psychologists look at the careers of the gifted, the smaller the role innate talent seems to play and the bigger the role preparation seems to play," he concludes.[3]

I cannot help but wonder if the same kind of devotion, dedication and diligence in those who push their plows is part of what God uses as a basis for greater mantles of promotion. Plowing in 3-D builds character, strengthens faith and engenders patience—because these practitioners serve God despite their fluctuating feelings and ongoing frustrations, regardless of circumstances and crises. They persevere when others turn back, give up, abandon their plows and run away. They may not be the most talented, most educated, most experienced or even the strongest. But they are the most faithful, loyal, determined—and stubborn.

Rather than being discouraged by the vast fields to be plowed before seeds can sprout and fruit can be harvested, these individuals start at the beginning of each new row and simply push their plows. Step by step, inch by inch, furrow by furrow, they upturn

3. Malcolm Gladwell, "Complexity and the Ten-Thousand-Hour Rule," *The New Yorker*, August 21, 2013, https://www.newyorker.com/sports/sporting-scene/complexity-and-the-ten-thousand-hour-rule.

the hard ground in order to fulfill their dreams. They keep going despite any obstacles blocking the path to progress.

People who love and serve God in the power of the Holy Spirit through the sacrifice of Jesus Christ work to discover their God-given purposes and steward His gifts to them, in much the same way as Elisha pushed his plow. They embody this truth: "Whatever you do, work heartily, as for the Lord and not for men, knowing that from the Lord you will receive the inheritance as your reward. You are serving the Lord Christ" (Colossians 3:23–24 ESV).

Such pushers of the plow know that not only do they persevere for the mantle of promotion awaiting them but also to reveal God's power in their lives. When we obediently and diligently serve without putting the focus on our own abilities, we let others glimpse the Lord working through us. We honor God by keeping our commitment to push our plows the same way we try to live our lives, for his glory. "So, whether you eat or drink, or whatever you do, do all to the glory of God" (1 Corinthians 10:31 ESV).

Storage Solutions

Many Millennials and young adults of Gen Z struggle with pushing their plows because they have been conditioned by overnight YouTube sensations and viral memes that turn their peers into social media celebrities. They are bright, talented, passionate and willing to work. But they are wary of wasting time and energy on any endeavor not promising guaranteed results. Members of our younger generations struggle to value diligence and devotion as virtues in their own right, and perhaps with good reason. Many of them are critical of the kind of corporate greed and capitalistic profiteering they have witnessed in their world.

This observation reminds us that the value of hard work must be determined not only by the plow-pusher's motivation but also by the results that such an investment of labor will produce. Without Spirit-led motives that seek to fulfill God-given dreams, our efforts are wasted. When greed causes us to push our plows for more, any harvest we reap will never be enough. Jesus made this clear in a parable about a wealthy plower whose work focused only on more for himself rather than for God and others:

> And he told them this parable: "The ground of a certain rich man yielded an abundant harvest. He thought to himself, 'What shall I do? I have no place to store my crops.'
>
> "Then he said, 'This is what I'll do. I will tear down my barns and build bigger ones, and there I will store my surplus grain. And I'll say to myself, "You have plenty of grain laid up for many years. Take life easy; eat, drink and be merry."'
>
> "But God said to him, 'You fool! This very night your life will be demanded from you. Then who will get what you have prepared for yourself?'
>
> "This is how it will be with whoever stores up things for themselves but is not rich toward God."
>
> Luke 12:16–21

Clearly, building bigger barns or renting more storage units is not the answer! The motive behind our willingness to push our plows each day matters, but it must be coupled with a meaningful goal. On another occasion, Jesus echoed the theme of this parable and asked us to examine what drives our ambitions: "What good is it for someone to gain the whole world, yet forfeit their soul?" (Mark 8:36). We can come up with a long list of successful, wealthy, high-octane movers and shakers who continue to strive for more because they are driven only by worldly motives and goals, not eternal ones for God's Kingdom. There are no storage solutions for what is inside the human heart other than trusting God and relying on the Holy Spirit.

Christ also told us, "Do not work for food that spoils, but for food that endures to eternal life, which the Son of Man will give you. For on him God the Father has placed his seal of approval" (John 6:27). As we assess the plows we are pushing, we must ask ourselves about both the motivation and the end result: Why are we doing the work we are doing? For whom? For what goals or results? Even criminals and terrorists work hard to fulfill their schemes, but their motivations—greed, power, vengeance—and their accomplishments—theft, murder, espionage—lead only to that which spoils.

Even something admirable like working to provide for one's family can become skewed if both the motive and the end result are not kept in mind. After a certain level of provision and security has been achieved, for instance, work can turn into an escape from engaging in actual relationships with family members. Most parents want to give their children more opportunities and advantages than they received, but without instilling the same work ethic in their offspring, parental sacrifices may backfire and create attitudes of entitlement.

The kind of plow-pushing that leads to mantles of promotion can have only one motivation: love, gratitude and trust in the living and almighty God. For children of God and followers of Jesus, our motivation originates in the relationship we have with our heavenly Father. Knowing that God sacrificed His only Son, and that Jesus gave His life for our sins, and that the Holy Spirit dwells within us, we discover that we desire only one worthy response for such gifts of salvation, redemption and eternal life: Our goal becomes a desire to give everything we are and everything we have in return.

The apostle Paul makes it clear that giving God all areas of our lives is an act of worship: "Therefore, I urge you, brothers and sisters, in view of God's mercy, to offer your bodies as a living sacrifice, holy and pleasing to God—this is your true and proper worship" (Romans 12:1). We push our plows as a sacrifice in order to honor the Lord more fully for what He has done, is doing and will do for us.

Outstanding in His Field

The Bible is filled with people chosen by God for daunting, seemingly impossible missions. From Abraham to Jacob, Ruth to Rahab, and Gideon to Esther, their stories reflect the way God's power and glory often shine through the unlikeliest of heroes. Despite their own lack of confidence, they trusted God for each step of their journeys. They were willing to serve, to push their plows, despite their inadequacies, insecurities and instabilities. And God used their willingness to trust Him to reveal His power.

We see a similar kind of trust, and willingness to push their respective plows, in the lives of Elijah and Elisha. We will explore the symbolic ways Elijah pushed his plow prior to meeting Elisha in the next chapter, but for now just know that he had to persevere through trials every bit as hard and rocky as the fields Elisha plowed. After the older prophet reaches one of the lowest points in his life, God meets him and sends him on a mission—to find Elisha.

Seeking his protégé and successor at God's direction, Elijah did not find his apprentice lounging under a shade tree. I am not implying any kind of judgment on taking time to relax! I simply find it significant that Elijah finds Elisha pushing a plow.

We know via the conduit of historical contextualization that as a farmer at this season Elisha would wake up, push the plow, break the ground and sow the seed. It is no coincidence that the man who pushed the plow ended up carrying the mantle. Plowing fields implies repetition in uniformed rows that follow a consistent pattern. Rhythm and fluidity are required in order to push through hard, rocky terrain or to navigate through soft, muddy ground. Plowing was tedious, strenuous work undertaken by those dedicated to the necessity of providing food not only for their own survival but for their families, tribes and communities.

In Elisha's day, plowing required mastery and control over beasts of burden, likely donkeys or, as Scripture indicates in this case, oxen. The sheer physicality of plowing required total body strength. Without a doubt, Elisha exerted his shoulders and upper body to hold and guide the plow handles while he maintained balance, control and speed with his torso, thighs, legs and feet. The job required focus as well to keep rows straight and animals pulling in tandem.

While I have never been a farmer, I have several friends who grew up on family farms. Most of them speak fondly of their memories, but none of them describes the work as anything less than exhausting. Getting up hours before dawn, they accepted physical labor as part of the process for sustaining their farm's productivity and their family's livelihood. There were animals to be fed, cows to be milked, horses to be trained, sheep to be herded, fences to be built and fields to be planted, weeded and harvested. Hard work was assumed, harkening back to the investment of their ancestors, who had been largely tied to an agricultural economy and a seasonal lifestyle.

Upon seeing the straining, sweating figure guiding a team of oxen to plow straight, even rows, Elijah surely must have been impressed. How could he not have admired the sheer physical force and focused attention on display? Perhaps it is similar to the admiration and respect we feel for those we see working hard and excelling in their particular lanes. It is the reaction I experience when I listen to a gifted up-and-coming preacher or when a lightning-fast runner dashes by me on a track or trail. I am often especially impressed when seeing someone doing something beyond my talent and skill set.

Elijah's response to his new prophetic partner also speaks volumes: He drapes his mantle over Elisha's shoulders. Like Samuel anointing David with holy oil to signify his selection as God's chosen king, this action symbolizes several transactions taking place. There is a generational passing of the torch from one servant-leader to another. There is also a kind of anointing from God's present prophet to the one the Lord has chosen to succeed him.

In addition, when Elijah's mantle falls on the man who has been pushing the plow, there is an invitation to a new season, a higher level, the next chapter. This invitation might also be interpreted as a kind of reward or recognition—not for plowing the longest time or the straightest rows but for Elisha's willingness to do the hard work God had placed before him.

You see, many people desire the mantle without ever pushing the plow. What they do not understand is that metaphorically and prophetically speaking, the mantle—a symbol of God's assignment, anointing and authority—only descends on those who faithfully push their plows.

Today's plow-pusher is tomorrow's mantle carrier.

Struggle to Steady

As I mentioned earlier, I wonder if the younger generations struggle more with patience to persevere with their plows because they are accustomed to the shortcuts afforded by technology. I realize such a broad generalization might sound old-fashioned or patronizing, and that is not my intent. I simply suspect that when people become accustomed to instant gratification in most areas of their lives, they then bristle when forced to work without a clear sense of when and how their long-term efforts will be rewarded.

Whether it is the cumulative impact of online culture and social media or simply our own impatience, most people have times when we struggle to steady our plows. Our circumstances affect both the work we are called to do and our attitude toward doing it. So wherever you find yourself right now, allow me to offer a few points you must embrace if you want to push the plow of perseverance in order to wear the mantle of greater responsibility.

We have noted this first point, but I want to stress it: There is a seasonal, sequential order to this progression. You must push the plow before you move on to carry the mantle. Otherwise, you may find yourself unprepared, ill-equipped or relying on your own power instead of God's. A hastily acquired mantle will not fit you or provide you with the covering you need to receive the anointing and to accomplish what you are called to do.

And here is the second point: You must not linger behind your plow when God reveals it is time to assume your mantle. It is often tempting to remain in the safety of the familiar rather than let go of the plow handles so that God can give you something new to hold.

And, to look at this from another angle, if your plows seem too heavy to bear or you feel weighted in place, then that can be another indication that you are holding on to a plow that God wants you to let go of. In other words, you might be doing something you were once called to do long after God has called you to move on. Whether out of fear or doubt or simply by not paying attention to the whisper of the Spirit, you cannot make forward progress if you hold on to a plow when your mantle is ready.

Do not get stuck behind a plow.

Do not get stuck behind past failures.

And do not get stuck behind past successes.

Thirdly, sometimes we become enamored of the plow. It is similar to feeling like a big fish in a little pond. Perhaps you enjoy the recognition or admiration that others show for the work you are doing. Pushing your plow, you can demonstrate and showcase your talents, abilities and strengths. But never allow your plow to define you.

Do not make the temporary permanent.

Do not mistake the process with the promise.

Do not confuse what you are going *through* with where you are going *to*.

And here is a fourth point: If you find yourself going through something you have never been through before, then it is only because you are about to step into what you have never stepped into before. If that sounds confusing, please read it again, slowly: If you have been pushing as you have never been pushing before, it is only because you are about to carry an anointing that you have never carried before.

You are in transition, moving from one mission to another. When you push the plow, you are breaking new ground and sowing new seed. When you wear the mantle, you are breaking new barriers and tending the harvest.

Elisha would wake up in the morning and resume the physically demanding job he agreed to do. No excuses, justifications, complaints or grumbling. If you have never pushed the plow, broken ground or sowed some seeds, then you lack the full capacity to understand what is required to fulfill this kind of dedication. But if you know what it is to push the plow, break the ground and sow a seed, then you know God has prepared you, continues to equip you and will empower you for more. Plow-pushers know their Master has a mantle for them!

When you push your plow like Elisha, then it means you live by faith every day. On good days and bad days, on rainy days and sunny days, on days when everyone loves you and on days when people hate you. On days when your bank account is full and on days when your ATM receipt makes fun of you. On days when you live off the gift and on all days when you survive only by His grace.

And when you live by faith each day, pushing your plow in whatever way, shape or form God has assigned you, then you can get ready. Because I am here to tell you—in the name of Jesus, with fear and trembling and an unbridled commitment to biblical orthodoxy and the centrality of Christ, not out of the womb of emotional exuberance or wishful thinking but driven by the Spirit of almighty God—I am here to tell you this: You will reap what you sow!

If you have been pushing the plow, breaking the ground and sowing the seed, then a mantle of more power, purpose and provision is about to fall on your shoulders. Whether you are a pastor or business entrepreneur, whether you are married or single, whether you are a creative leader or a faithful follower, whether you are mentoring your biological children or your "spiritual" children into God's purposes, in whatever fashion you remain a committed steward steering your plow, there is more for you. Some days you may be pushing your plow with a smile on your face, and some days with tears rolling down your cheeks. Some days it may seem as if the windows of heaven have opened before you, and some days you feel sure that the powers of hell have been unleashed to stop you. In all of these things, you have pushed through and persevered with your plow.

If you know what I am talking about, if you can feel tears forming in your eyes as you read these words, if you believe that no one knows how hard you have been pushing your plow, if you cannot understand why you are still pushing the same plow after so many years, then get ready, my friend. Get ready because . . .

There is a prophetic mantle, a fresh touch from heaven coming your way.

There is a heavenly deposit, a new anointing coming your way.

There is a favorable shift in your atmosphere coming your way.

There are blessings, resources and harvests coming your way.

There is unbridled, unparalleled and unprecedented favor coming your way.

The prophet Elisha is not remembered predominately as the man with the plow, but rather as the man who inherited a mantle of a greater portion. Just so, you will not be defined by what you push; you will be defined by what you carry.

Catch Your Breath

When you have been pushing your plow for a long time, or at least what feels like a very long time, then it is natural to grow weary. You keep doing the same things day after day, and even though others depend on you, they might not show their support or appreciation. You may begin to feel overlooked and taken for granted—or worse, used and exploited. You may be juggling multiple responsibilities and feeling pulled from one plow to another.

Eventually, the weight of your plow becomes heavier and more unwieldy. Your body, tired and exhausted, rebels against the schedule you keep. You persevere but you are beginning to lose perspective, allowing emotions of anger, resentment, frustration, loneliness and insignificance to overwhelm you. Still, you get up each and every day and go to your plow, doing your best to put your feelings aside in order to keep your commitment. It is even possible that you have slipped into depression and feel stuck in place, on a treadmill of plowing, plowing, plowing with no end in sight.

If this describes your experience as a plow-pusher, then take a moment to catch your breath, my faithful friend. And then remember another pair of truths from God's Word. First, keep in mind what Jesus told His followers:

> "Come to me, all you who are weary and burdened, and I will give you rest. Take my yoke upon you and learn from me, for I am gentle and humble in heart, and you will find rest for your souls. For my yoke is easy and my burden is light."
>
> Matthew 11:28–30

While pushing our plows may never seem as easy or light as we may wish, Jesus made it clear that we are to follow His example and rest in the spiritual peace of the Holy Spirit.

Here is a truth that I encourage you to keep front and center: No matter how you feel or who overlooks the ground where you plow, you must know that your heavenly Father sees you and values you. The Bible tells us, "Don't allow yourselves to be weary or disheartened in planting good seeds, for the season of reaping the wonderful harvest you've planted is coming!" (Galatians 6:9 TPT). Your Creator designed you for a special and specific purpose. Even if you feel ready for your mantle before it is given, take heart and remain patient.

God has not forgotten you and will never abandon you.

You will soon be carrying the mantle of new challenges, new goals, new resources.

Get ready for a holy deposit of God's grace and power that will enable you to magnify the name of Jesus as you have never magnified it before!

Push Your Plow, Meet Your Mantle

Once again, you will find questions below to assist you in your absorption of this chapter's biblical truths and application to your life. Please consider them as a way to personalize your experience of pushing your plow and meeting the mantle of promotion God has for you. I believe you will find it beneficial to jot down your answers so that you can return to them for review as you progress through this book.

A brief prayer is provided to help you connect with God about what you have learned here. I encourage you to take a few moments to wait in stillness and silence before Him, to quiet your mind and then to unburden your heart. Remember that He knows exactly what you are facing right now and is measuring you for a mantle of promotion that will fit you like a glove.

1. What would you identify as your primary plow, or the main focus of your God-given responsibilities, at this point in your life? How would you describe the way you push your plow on a daily basis?

2. What challenges you the most about continuing to serve faithfully with your present plowing? Impatience? Weariness? Busyness? Boredom? Resentment? Something else? What obstacles and circumstantial barriers get in the way?

3. How has God sustained you and provided what you need in order to persevere with your plowing? What mantle of promotion might He be preparing for you? What makes you think so?

Dear Lord, thank You for the talents, abilities and skills You have instilled in me. I praise You as well for the many blessings of experience, wisdom and provision You have bestowed on me in the midst of pushing my plow. Grant me patience so that I may persevere and wait on Your timing rather than rushing ahead or lagging behind. Guide and direct my steps each day as I try to be the best steward I can be of Your resources. Keep my grip firm on the plow and my rows straight as I rely on Your Holy Spirit as the source of my strength and stamina. I pray with the psalmist, "May the favor of the Lord our God rest on us; establish the work of our hands for us—yes, establish the work of our hands" (Psalm 90:17). Amen.

3

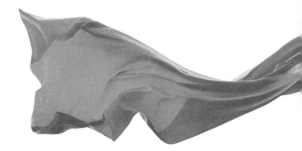

The Mantle of Power, Patience and Provision

During times of drought, plow with patience and persistence as God miraculously provides for all your needs!

Someone who had been blessed by our church once gave me the gift of a custom-made, hand-tailored suit as a way of expressing appreciation. I wondered if the person was subtly suggesting that my wardrobe needed help or simply knew this was an indulgence that I would not splurge on! I accepted graciously and made an appointment at the men's shop, a discreetly hidden little storefront in a gentrified area near downtown, and had no idea what to expect.

Inside the shop I felt as if I had stepped back in time, returning to the turn of the twentieth century, when every gentleman owned at least one fine suit, and often only one suit, for weddings, funerals and special occasions. The place had oak paneling and high ceilings, a faded Turkish rug gracing the hardwood floor, and built-in shelves covering an entire wall with bolt after bolt of fabric stacked like giant books. The sartorial little shop even smelled manly and old-fashioned with the blended scent of bay rum, leather and cedar.

Based on the surroundings, I expected the tailor to be a silver-haired gentleman in a three-piece suit with a pocket watch and British accent.

Instead, a young Latino man emerged from the back room wearing jeans, suede kicks, earbuds and what appeared to be a lab coat with lots of pockets. "*Hola!*" he said with a broad smile. "You must be Pastor Sam. A pleasure to meet you!"

My new friend introduced himself as Emilio. He then asked me to describe the kind of suit I would like, both in terms of what I envisioned and the purposes it would serve for various occasions. When I told him I had not really thought about it, he made it clear that I was going to start thinking about it very carefully.

Did I want a classic, more traditional suit, like something I could wear to the White House? Or maybe something a little hipper and more stylish for when I took my wife out for a nice dinner? Did I prefer a dark, neutral color or something fresher and less predictable? Solid, striped, plaid? Would I be traveling in it and need something synthetic and less prone to wrinkling? Or would this be for special occasions only, which would allow for natural wool blends?

My expert guide then proceeded to explain the process and the multitude of choices available and decisions to be made for my new suit. While I am a strong believer in the adage that God is in the details, I had no idea just how many holy details go into making a man's jacket and pair of pants. Eva had offered to accompany me, but aligning our schedules proved challenging, so I thanked her and said, "How hard can it be, right?"

Emilio proved a godsend. He guided me toward an Italian blended wool fabric, navy with subtle lighter-blue pinstripes. From there, he showed me various finished suits and let me point to the details I wanted for my own. Pockets, lapels, cuffs, buttons, buttonholes—I even got to choose the fabric for the lining!

With his apprentice helping, Emilio then took my measurements and told me my new suit would be ready in four to six weeks. While I thought the process that afternoon had taken a long time, I realized that that was nothing compared to the actual cutting, assembling and sewing the two matching garments. Ordering online usually promises quick gratification with two-day delivery, but a suit made just for me apparently required almost two months.

Just when I had almost forgotten about my suit, Emilio called to inform me it was ready. As excited as a kid on Christmas morning, I could not wait to see the finished product—and I was not disappointed. My new suit proved as comfortable as my favorite jeans and sweatshirt. Emilio and his staff marveled at their creation. It fit me perfectly.

All those details Emilio had pressed me to choose paid off: It was neither too loose nor too tight; neither too stiff nor too soft. I could not believe how much better these garments fit than what I was used to wearing. Needless to say, I feel a surge of confidence wearing this suit that I have never experienced with my usual off-the-rack brands. Which is only natural, after all, because this suit was made for me and me alone. There is not another one like it in the world.

While I remain grateful for the generous gift from my benefactor, I share this experience with you to make this point: God's mantle of promotion for your life requires time in order to give you a perfect fit, but it is more than worth the wait. God is the ultimate benefactor of blessings, and His gifts are always tailor-made for your life!

Ravens to the Rescue

When you have finished a season of plowing and are ready for promotion, you never have to worry about how your mantle will fit.

God has designed your particular mantle for you and you alone, including all you bring—talents, gifts, abilities, experiences—so that it covers every area of your life. Your blessings are bespoke and your garments of praise proclaim God's glory! The King of kings has chosen you to be co-heir with His Son, Jesus Christ, and to be filled with His Holy Spirit. When you experience the fullness of this supernatural relationship, you are more than willing to plow faithfully and wait patiently for your mantle of promotion.

While Elisha's service involved literally pushing his plow and planting seeds in order to receive his mantle of promotion, Elijah's plow-pushing involved persevering through extreme weather, confrontations with idolaters, miraculous moments, death threats and debilitating depression. You see, prior to following God's instructions to find, anoint and mentor Elisha, the prophet Elijah experienced a series of supernatural adventures rivaling any sci-fi novel or superhero movie. Metaphorically, each incident provided more material—more fabric—for the mantle already draping the prophet's shoulders, requiring Elijah to trust God, wait on God, be empowered by God and used by God.

With wicked idolaters Ahab and Jezebel encouraging their subjects to bow before the pagan gods Baal and Asherah, God used Elijah to get their attention. The Lord spoke through His prophet to remind the people of Israel of His divine power and holy authority as the one true God, Creator of heaven and earth. But with the king and queen determined to mock God and kill Elijah, the communication process was never going to be easy.

The confrontation began when Elijah declared to Ahab, "As the Lord, the God of Israel, lives, whom I serve, there will be neither dew nor rain in the next few years except at my word" (1 Kings 17:1). Water is essential, of course, to sustain life—plants, animals, people—and a drought would bring the agriculturally based nation to its knees. Interestingly enough, though, Elijah and others who still worshiped God were also forced to endure this deadly dry season.

As evidenced by Elijah's experience, however, God remained faithful and provided for the needs of those who continued to serve Him. The Lord told His prophet to go camp in the Kerith Ravine, east of the Jordan River, where Elijah would receive sustenance. Sure enough, once he was there, "the ravens brought him bread and meat in the morning and bread and meat in the evening, and he drank from the brook" (1 Kings 17:6). Long before Grubhub, God was delivering 100-percent-organic food and drink for His children!

Mantle of Miracles

When the brook eventually ran dry, God directed Elijah to go to Zarephath, where he would meet a widow with provisions. There, at the town gate, the prophet saw a woman gathering sticks for a fire and asked her for a drink of water as well as some bread to eat (see 1 Kings 17:10–11). Before we consider this woman's response, keep in mind that these were dire times; water and food were likely more precious than silver and gold. So when a stranger asked this lady to give away the small portion of life-giving commodities she possessed, it seems only human that she hesitated:

> "As surely as the Lord your God lives," she replied, "I don't have any bread—only a handful of flour in a jar and a little olive oil in

a jug. I am gathering a few sticks to take home and make a meal for myself and my son, that we may eat it—and die."

Elijah said to her, "Don't be afraid. Go home and do as you have said. But first make a small loaf of bread for me from what you have and bring it to me, and then make something for yourself and your son. For this is what the LORD, the God of Israel, says: 'The jar of flour will not be used up and the jug of oil will not run dry until the day the LORD sends rain on the land.'"

She went away and did as Elijah had told her. So there was food every day for Elijah and for the woman and her family. For the jar of flour was not used up and the jug of oil did not run dry, in keeping with the word of the LORD spoken by Elijah.

1 Kings 17:12–16

Notice the amount of information contained in the widow's reply. First, she began by calling on the name of the living God, identifying herself as one who had not abandoned her faith. Next, she made her dire situation vividly clear. She anticipated that the meager meal she was about to make would be her last. If we unite the latter fact with the former truth, we see the response of those who live in the tension between their trust in God and the difficult facts before them.

We see evidence of this woman's faith even before the prophet arrived. When Elijah first spotted her she was gathering sticks for the fire to bake her last tiny loaf of bread. Rather than despair, this woman did what she could. She had no expectation for more and knew logically she and her son were on the brink of death. Nonetheless, she did not give up hope!

Further evidence for the widow's faith emerged after Elijah told her to go use what she had to bake bread, first for him and then for herself and her son. And then the prophet, speaking on behalf of the Lord, declared something that must have required a major leap of faith for this poor woman: "The jar of flour will not be used up and the jug of oil will not run dry until the day the LORD sends rain on the land" (1 Kings 17:14). Can you imagine what she must have felt in that moment?

Surely, she experienced some flicker of doubt, skepticism, wariness or fear, or all of these at once. After all, Elijah was a stranger to her! And now he not only had the audacity to ask her for food but persisted even after she told him she had almost none left. Even more amazing than his culinary directive, Elijah told her that she would not run out of flour and oil for as long as the drought persisted.

So what did she do? She went home and did as instructed. And God kept the promise made through His prophet by providing enough not only to feed Elijah but her family as well. One moment she was gathering sticks to bake her last meal, and the next she was living in the miraculous provision of a faithful God.

When we patiently persist in our plowing, the Lord's mantle of miracles sustains us.

Limitations of Loss

Elijah's relationship with his divinely appointed hostess could easily have ended there. Her faithfulness was tested, she persevered in pushing her plow, and God miraculously provided a mantle to cover her during the drought. But the widow's story, at least what we are told about it here, did not conclude with her bread baking. Instead, she had to keep plowing in the face of perhaps the most devastating experience any person can know—the death of a dearly loved child.

We are not told how much time had passed, only that "some time later" the widow's son became ill and grew worse until he died (1 Kings 17:17). In the depth of her loss, this mother's question to Elijah reflects the emotional trajectory we often experience in the midst of overwhelming grief: powerlessness, followed by guilt and concluding with the temptation to blame God. "What do you have against me, man of God?" the widow asked Elijah. "Did you come to remind me of my sin and kill my son?" (1 Kings 17:18).

Apparently, she assumed that if this prophet of God could save her life with a miracle, then he could also take away life with such divine power. Or maybe she thought that after God had saved her life and that of her son through Elijah that they were entitled to a kind of divine protection with anointed immune systems. Either way, this woman's perspective was limited by the constraints of her human understanding caused by losing her son.

Can you relate? Have you suffered while plowing and doubted God's goodness?

We often rush into the same kinds of doubts, questions and fears when times get hard and something unexpected happens. We are going along, pushing our plows and making sure our rows are neat and our seeds get planted. If we are serving God obediently, then should not our circumstances go smoothly? Should not the weather remain pleasant and the skies clear? And should not the children we love and pray for thrive and be protected as well?

As much as God loves us, nowhere in the Bible does He promise to make our lives problem-free. Because He gave us free will, meaning we can rebel against Him—note the state of our fallen world—we are forced to live in the consequences of our sinful, selfish decisions. God is always present in our midst and willing to hear our prayers, but we must sacrifice our own designs and desires in order to serve Him. He asks us to trust that He knows best despite what our senses, minds and hearts may tell us. While we are not free from trials and tribulations, we are free from having to endure them and overcome them in our own power.

Jesus reminded His followers that our Father in heaven "causes his sun to rise on the evil and the good, and sends rain on the righteous and the unrighteous" (Matthew 5:45). When we welcome Christ into our hearts, accept the free gift of salvation through His sacrifice on the cross and live in the power of the Holy Spirit, we begin a process of spiritual transformation usually called sanctification. We are still sinful human beings even though God has forgiven our sins and is at work in our lives. This side of heaven we are a work in progress: not totally perfected like Jesus, but not stuck on the treadmill of selfish idolatry.

We must exercise patience while pushing our plows if we want to experience the power of promotion that comes with our mantles.

Never Too Late

Rather than answer the widow's desperate questions directly, Elijah went immediately into action:

> "Give me your son," Elijah replied. He took him from her arms, carried him to the upper room where he was staying, and laid him on his bed. Then he cried out to the LORD, "LORD my God, have you brought tragedy even on this widow I am staying with, by causing her son to die?" Then he stretched himself out on the boy three times and cried out to the LORD, "LORD my God, let this boy's life return to him!"
>
> The LORD heard Elijah's cry, and the boy's life returned to him, and he lived. Elijah picked up the child and carried him down

from the room into the house. He gave him to his mother and said, "Look, your son is alive!"

1 Kings 17:19–23

This incredible scene reminds me of a similar miracle performed hundreds of years later when Jesus brought His friend Lazarus back to life (see John 11:1–44). In both situations, the families experienced regret, confusion and unbearable grief as they came to grips with the fact that it was too late, that the sick family member had actually died, that God was somehow to blame. Lazarus's sisters, Mary and Martha, had sent word to Jesus that their brother was sick, likely dying, but Jesus continued ministering to others, following His Father's pace rather than heeding the sisters' urgent plea to come right away.

When Jesus finally arrived, Lazarus had been dead four days and was already entombed. Both sisters, upon seeing the Messiah, said to Him, "Lord, if you had been here, my brother would not have died" (John 11:21, 32). Perhaps they expected Jesus, as their friend, to rush to them in order to save their brother's life. After Christ failed to live up to their expectations, their faith wavered. Surely, if He really cared about them, wouldn't Jesus have come right away? And if He really was the Son of God, as they believed, then wouldn't He have saved their brother?

Human logic and experience indicated that the opportunity to restore this life had passed. When Jesus wept at news of his friend's death, it raised questions that some scholars and theologians continue to enjoy debating today. Why did Jesus not arrive sooner? And why cry if He was about to raise Lazarus from the dead?

I believe that our answers are found in what happens next—not only the miracle Jesus performed but the way He performed it. Arriving at the cave used as a tomb, Christ ordered the stone to be rolled away. Martha cautioned Him, "But, Lord, . . . by this time there is a bad odor, for he has been there four days" (John 11:39). Her warning was practical and, once again, based on the logical human perception that decay of the body was inevitable. Jesus, however, challenged her assumption before doing what seemed utterly impossible:

> Then Jesus said, "Did I not tell you that if you believe, you will see the glory of God?"
>
> So they took away the stone. Then Jesus looked up and said, "Father, I thank you that you have heard me. I knew that you always hear me, but I said this for the benefit of the people standing here, that they may believe that you sent me."
>
> When he had said this, Jesus called in a loud voice, "Lazarus, come out!" The dead man came out, his hands and feet wrapped with strips of linen, and a cloth around his face.
>
> Jesus said to them, "Take off the grave clothes and let him go."
>
> John 11:40–44

Jesus called on His Father, not because He lacked the power Himself—because, after all, He is the Son of God—but because He wanted those gathered to give His Father the glory. To know that God was, is and will be His power source. To witness first-hand that nothing is impossible for the living God!

Similarly, Elijah knew that God's power was no match for death. He pleaded with his heavenly Father to have mercy on this widow who had demonstrated kindness, obedience and hospitality. God heard the prophet's prayers and breathed life into the boy, resulting in the grateful mother's exclamation: "Now I know that you are a man of God and that the word of the LORD from your mouth is the truth" (1 Kings 17:24).

In both situations, human perceptions, limitations and expectations caused people to question God or outright blame Him for their devastating loss. They failed to trust God's ability to do the impossible, to restore life in place of death, to transform a trial into a triumph. But when we rely on the Lord's power, it is never too late to do the impossible.

Dress for Success

Elijah's mantle, the same cloak he would soon drape over his anointed apprentice, Elisha, was not simply a cape-like piece of fabric worn for practical reasons. Yes, such a garment provided protection against the elements of sun, rain and wind as well as dust storms during the drought. The cloak also warmed its wearer on chilly nights when the temperature plummeted in the desert. Multifunctional, the mantle worn by Elijah could be a blanket, pillow, tent, shelter, towel, robe and headdress.

Beyond these practical benefits, however, Elijah's mantle embodied and represented the prophetic spiritual authority bestowed on him by God. This mantle was on him, literally and spiritually, when the prophet exercised holy authority and unleashed a drought on the wayward nation of Israel and its idolatrous leaders (see 1 Kings 17:1). The prophetic mantle of power, patience and provision was all he needed to dress for success!

This mantle of miraculous power was on Elijah when he hid in the ravine next to the brook where ravens brought him food. When the brook dried up, Elijah gathered his mantle and followed God's direction to the widow in Zarephath, whose flour and oil never ran out. After the widow's son became ill and died, the prophet's mantle became a prayer shawl as he cried out to the

Lord for healing power to restore the boy's life. Later, as we will explore in the next chapter, Elijah's mantle covered him when he called down fire from heaven and then cried out, "Here comes the rain!" (see 1 Kings 18:36–38, 41–45).

No matter what Elijah experienced, he wore his mantle of God's prophetic power and mighty miracles. He knew what we must always remember: The God of the process is the God of the outcome. We must not confuse the temporary with the permanent, the momentary with the eternal. God wants to enlarge our perspectives so that we trust Him with our present circumstances as well as our uncertain futures. When the path we expected to unfold suddenly takes a detour or leads to a dead end, we must not rush to question and doubt God rather than reconsider our expectations.

Remember: Do not mistake what you are going *through* with where you are going *to*!

If you have been through at least one spiritual, relational or financial drought in your life, then keep going. If you have been through many such droughts of disappointment, distraction and derailment, then keep going faster. If you have been in a drought so long that your Instagram account pops up when I Google the word *drought*, then God bless you!

Jesus told His followers that not only would they encounter trials but that they should plan to walk a rocky path if they wanted to follow His example:

> "If the world hates you, keep in mind that it hated me first. If you belonged to the world, it would love you as its own. As it is, you do not belong to the world, but I have chosen you out of the world. That is why the world hates you. Remember what I told you: 'A servant is not greater than his master.' If they persecuted

me, they will persecute you also. If they obeyed my teaching, they will obey yours also."

John 15:18–20

Others' perceptions of who we are and what we stand for might change. Our circumstances will likely change. But with God there are no "shifting shadows" (James 1:17). He is our solid rock, our immoveable foundation, our steady anchor when everything else may flip upside down. Even as we press onward and upward, diligently pushing our plows, we can count on God's prophetic mantle of power, purpose, protection—and we can be sure that it will always fit like a glove!

As God's messenger to the disobedient people of Israel, Elijah proclaimed a deadly drought, performed miracles for meals, brought the dead back to life, summoned fire in a competitive supernatural showdown, and unleashed life-giving rain from above. Through it all, he trusted God as his power source.

We are called to do the same. Your mantle's heavenly origin does not mean that you will not experience trials, temptations and tempests. It does mean, however, that God will equip and empower you to push through them. And with each storm you endure and each obstacle you overcome, the power and patience you exhibit will add new provision—new fabric—to your mantle to accommodate the growing strength of your faith.

Spiritual Security Blanket

As you grow stronger in your faith, you will discover that God's mantle is the ultimate security blanket for your soul. Your mantle reminds you of where you have been and where you are going. Woven from your life's experiences, it is stitched by God's loving purpose for your time on this earth. Your mantle is your testimony of God's faithfulness in your life; it is your trophy of His triumph over all your trials.

When our children were little, they often had some blanket, stuffed animal or toy that gave them comfort, security and assurance. Just like Charlie Brown's friend Linus in the *Peanuts* cartoons, they carried their symbolic security blankets with them wherever they went. Heaven forbid that we forgot to bring them when traveling to visit relatives or, worse, lost one of them on a trip to the playground. Those fleece blankets, teddy bears, plush Disney characters, action figures and favorite storybooks provided something ongoing and familiar, a handrail to grab when the ground felt shaky and a lifeline to hold on to when circumstances jarred them.

As kids mature they generally grow out of the need to cling to their teddy bears. Many adults, however, would be surprised to discover that they are equally attached to possessions or abilities as their own adult-sized security blankets. In other words, their emotional lifelines are found in something rather than in God. For some people, it might be grown-up toys like sports cars, boats and ATVs. For others, security is found in the identity of being someone who enjoys certain hobbies, collects special treasures or travels to exotic destinations.

There is nothing wrong with any of these pursuits or possessions—only in how we regard them. Because if we rely on money, power and material objects to define us and their acquisition to assure us, then we are guilty of the same practices as Ahab, Jezebel and the wayward people of Israel. Basically, we are worshiping idols just as they did. Ours are probably not called Baal and Asherah, but they are idols just the same.

God is the only One who can give us the ultimate security and absolute certainty we long to know. The Bible assures us that

"Jesus Christ is the same yesterday and today and forever" (Hebrews 13:8 ESV). He alone is "the author and finisher of our faith" (Hebrews 12:2 NKJV), our Creator who will finish the good work He has started in our lives (see Philippians 1:6). We can pray joyfully and confidently the words of the psalmist:

> If you say, "The LORD is my refuge," and you make the Most High your dwelling, no harm will overtake you, no disaster will come near your tent. For he will command his angels concerning you to guard you in all your ways; they will lift you up in their hands, so that you will not strike your foot against a stone.
>
> Psalm 91:9–12

When we walk with God and wear His mantle over our lives, then we have no need of anything the world offers. No earthly security blanket compares with the eternal assurance of God's love—in this life and the life to come. So like Elisha, push your plow as you persevere with diligence, and like Elijah, wear your mantle with full authority of your prophetic power through the Spirit of the living God!

Push Your Plow, Meet Your Mantle

Once again, below are a few questions to help you reflect on this chapter and apply it to your life. It is not homework so much as *life*work. While it may require more time, writing down your responses provides a good way to chart your progress as you persevere in pushing your plow and embracing God's prophetic mantle of power, patience and provision.

Regardless of what you write down, I urge you to unplug and find a quiet place where you can enjoy at least ten minutes without interruption. Still your heart before God, surrendering all your worries, cares and concerns to His keeping. Ask the Holy Spirit to guide you as you consider each question, and then spend the remaining time in prayer.

1. When have you blamed God for hard circumstances or painful losses? How did you get through those experiences? What did you learn from them about yourself? About God?

2. What season of your life has been most prone to a spiritual drought? In other words, when have you struggled to trust God and walk by faith because of the fear, uncertainty and doubt resulting from unexpected events or painful relationships?

3. When has God provided "flour and oil" for you during times of hardship? How did His provision allow you to persevere in your plowing? How did it shape your expectations about how He continues to provide for you?

Heavenly Father, I give You thanks and praise for the ways You continue to sustain me in the midst of circumstances that often leave me weary and discouraged. I know that trusting You and following Jesus does not mean that I will never struggle and suffer in this life. But I also know that You always equip and empower me with all I need to follow You. Give me strength, stamina and courage so that I can let go of my false idols and worldly security blankets. Your mantle is all I need, Lord, so help me to remember that You are always with me and Your hand is always on my life. I trust You and want always to serve You with all that You have entrusted to me. Amen.

4

The Mantle of Holy Confrontation

Your path out of drought into refreshing rain will take you through the fire, but the power of God's truth will always expose the impotence of idols!

Trusting God means putting your best face forward.

This is the amazing lesson a little girl once taught me about the true meaning of confrontation. This was years ago, when my wife, Eva, and I were filling in for one of the preschoolers' Sunday school classes at our church. Our own kids were quite young then, and one of them was also in the class. Our lesson that morning was on Daniel in the lions' den, but what I learned applies equally to Elijah's showdown with King Ahab as well as the enemies you and I face today.

After reading the Bible story of how Daniel refused to stop praying to God and, therefore, broke the king's law (see Daniel 6), I helped Eva get the little ones seated around the table. She showed them several illustrations of Daniel facing the lions and then asked the kids to draw their own pictures of what they imagined it was like. I remember one little boy ended up drawing a scene that depicted a stick-figure Daniel shooting a dozen snarling lions, all in various anguished positions of violent defeat and massive blood loss. I suspected that he relied more on a jungle safari video game than our actual text that morning.

Another child colored a picture that showed Daniel as lion tamer, looking more like a ringmaster than a captive prophet in Babylon. Someone else's illustration showed Daniel with a lion, closely resembling Clifford the Big Red Dog, on a leash, both smiling as they strolled along in a room with a couch, chairs and a big TV.

"Is this Daniel's house?" Eva asked the little girl.

"No," she replied, "just his den. It's what we call our living room."

Then as I casually strolled around the table, I spied one little girl, who had already proved to be quite opinionated, coloring her entire piece of paper with a giant face. Her Daniel had long dark hair, big blue eyes and an expression bordering on a defiant, smug sneer.

"I like your Daniel," I said, smiling in encouragement. "But where are the lions?"

She looked up at me as if I were the saddest, least imaginative, dullest person she had ever encountered. "Daniel confronted them and they ran away."

I nodded. "So he just prayed and stared them down?"

She glanced up at me in disbelief, as if she could not understand how I could be both a grown-up *and* a pastor and not know this.

"Trusting God means putting your best face forward!" she said.

"You mean your best foot forward?" I said gently, assuming I was correcting her figure of speech.

She put down her crayon. "No, Pastor Sam, if you start walking before it's time, you could hurt your foot! When you're having a bad day, you pray and put your best *face* forward. You scare the devil and show everybody that it's not so bad because God loves you and will take care of you."

From the mouths of babes, right? I was speechless.

I pondered her explanation for some time, wondering who had taught her this response to facing, literally, unexpected challenges. Over the years since then, I am not sure I have ever heard a better definition of holy confrontation. I had never considered Daniel's expression and attitude in regard to spending the night in the lions' den, or if I had, I assumed he was as fearful and anxious as I would have been. But this little girl clearly had a different vision of what his defiant faith looked like.

Whenever I believe God calls me to wear the mantle of holy confrontation, I remember the expression on Daniel's face in her picture. So often, people tend to tilt toward extremes when confronting others about matters on which they disagree or share conflict. Many hate the uncomfortable tension of clashing with others and try to avoid confrontation at any cost. Others seem to thrive on the drama of confronting others and showing them their mistakes.

Neither of these extremes, however, reflects the courage, confidence and character required to stand up for God in the face of adversity. Throughout my life I have often found myself in positions that required me to confront people who have so much more— more power, more intelligence, more money, more authority—than I do. At various times I have been led by God to confront elected officials in the community, business owners with considerable clout, angry members of my congregation, international ministry leaders, and even presidents from both major political parties in the White House! Yes, I have been compelled by the Holy Spirit to speak God's truth to a president of the United States—more than once!

My desire each time I am called to engage in holy confrontation is to advance God's Kingdom and to uphold His truth. I never confront another person in anger or, to the best of my human ability, to advance my own agenda. When I have confronted political leaders and presidents of both parties, I have maintained my devotion to only one cause—not the "donkey's" or the "elephant's" cause but the Lamb's! I cannot say that I enjoyed any of those sometimes tense, often emotionally charged conversations. But each one forced me to rely on God and the power of the Holy Spirit just a little more.

Or, as that young lady phrased it years ago, to trust God and put my best face forward.

You and I, as God's people, are called to respect and obey governmental authority, but we also answer to a Higher Authority. Ultimately, we serve the King of kings and Lord of lords in all that we do. You have been called to be salt and light in every situation where God places you—your home, your work, your church. You and I must be willing to confront when God calls us to do so.

Helping the Helpless

During those challenging seasons of confrontation I prayed without ceasing for God's guidance, wisdom and understanding. I sought to emulate the only perfect person who has ever walked this earth, my Lord and Savior, Jesus Christ. And I relied on the supernatural power of the Holy Spirit to work through me and others in order to accomplish what He had called us to do.

Perhaps you have been in a similar situation: If you did not speak up about an injustice, no one else was going to. Perhaps you have been challenged in your employment, where the voices of those who are being wronged are also being ignored. Or maybe your church family has missed the mark and slid into a stance that is clearly immoral. Maybe even in your family a biblical truth is being ignored and poisoning the sanctity of your home.

If this is happening to you, I want to show you how you, too, can draw strength and inspiration from the example of Elijah, who demonstrated the courage required to wear the mantle of holy confrontation.

Holy Trouble

The political, social and cultural divisiveness in our nations and our world requires us to stand apart from the majority, to go against the powerful and to confront the privileged. Now perhaps more than ever, we are called to act on behalf of the poor, the weak, the defenseless, the disenfranchised, the orphans and the widows. To stand up for what we believe, for what we know is right, for the truth found in the living Word of God. But standing up for the truth is rarely comfortable, convenient or convivial.

It is so much easier to go with the flow, to back away from the battle, to look the other way. Even when immorality, greed, perversion, murder and idolatry assault our lives on a daily basis, we may be reluctant to voice opposition because there will be a price to pay, consequences to contend with and changes to make. We risk being "unfriended" and "unliked" on social media, being criticized and chastised by opponents who do not even know what and whom we stand for.

In our divisive world of political animosity and civil unrest, we often allow the mantle of holy confrontation to fall from our shoulders. Rather than speak up for what is right in the eyes of God, we hold our tongues in order to conform to the consensus. Instead of calling out injustice, unrighteousness, immorality and idolatry, we avoid rocking the boat.

Whether we are intimidated by a cultural climate of cancellations and criticism or fear the fallout from standing firm in our faith, we must muster the courage of Elijah, who confronted King Ahab. You will recall that God's prophet had declared that rain would not fall, a way of commanding everyone's attention by suffering the consequences of a life-threatening famine, a season Elijah and others survived only through the provision and protection of God.

As the famine stretched into its third year, God told Elijah that it was time for a more direction confrontation: "Go and present yourself to Ahab, and I will send rain on the land" (1 Kings 18:1). Elijah set off immediately to see the king, but before reaching him, the prophet encountered Ahab's palace administrator, Obadiah, identified as "a devout believer in the LORD" (verse 3) who had worshiped the Lord since his youth (see verse 12). As evidence of his faithfulness, Obadiah had hidden a hundred prophets in two caves, providing them with food and water, and protecting them from Jezebel's murderous intent.

Elijah instructed Obadiah to go tell the king that the prophet would meet him face to face. The faithful Obadiah, however, was fearful of his master's wrath concerning the prophet.

"No problem," Elijah basically replied. "I'll tell him myself!"

Ahab, upon seeing his least favorite person approaching, greeted Elijah with these words: "Is that you, you troubler of Israel?" (verse 17).

Ahab was saying, "What do you want, you big troublemaker?" And I cannot help but wonder if this is a more polite translation of the mocking rage embedded in the original language.

Regardless, Elijah deflected the accusation into a true reflection of the situation: "I have not made trouble for Israel. . . . But you and your father's family have. You have abandoned the

LORD's commands and have followed the Baals" (verse 18). In other words, "I'm not the problem—you're the problem!"

When we exercise the mantle of holy confrontation, we may also be viewed as a troublemaker, an instigator, a catalyst for change when everyone around us wants the status quo. Our opponents may call us names or try to influence others so that they, too, will align against us. Our adversaries hope that if they convince others that we are the cause of problems, then we will be silenced.

That is when we must dare to start holy trouble.

Spiritual Showdown

As if to prove his point about the true source of Israel's problems, Elijah then told Ahab to gather everyone for a holy confrontation on Mount Carmel. Once they were assembled, Elijah gave an ultimatum—to the people of Israel, their king and queen, and their bogus collection of pagan gods:

> Elijah went before the people and said, "How long will you waver between two opinions? If the LORD is God, follow him; but if Baal is God, follow him."
>
> But the people said nothing.
>
> Then Elijah said to them, "I am the only one of the LORD's prophets left, but Baal has four hundred and fifty prophets. Get two bulls for us. Let Baal's prophets choose one for themselves, and let them cut it into pieces and put it on the wood but not set fire to it. I will prepare the other bull and put it on the wood but not set fire to it. Then you call on the name of your god, and I will call on the name of the LORD. The god who answers by fire—he is God."
>
> 1 Kings 18:21–24

As you can see, either Elijah set himself up to be humiliated in one of the most dramatic displays ever, or he created an impossible underdog scenario for himself in which only God could ignite the sacrifice on His altar.

And Elijah was just getting started! Not only did the 450 prophets of Baal pray and chant all morning without a hint of a spark near their sacrificial altar, but when Elijah began to taunt them they shouted louder and slashed themselves with swords until evening. Embarrassed by their god's lack of response, the false prophets and spectators then watched in awe as Elijah proved his point.

Before Elijah prayed for God to burn the sacrificial offering, the prophet repaired the altar of the Lord, dug a trench around it, arranged the sacrifice and called for four large jugs of water to be poured over the carcass of the bull, the wood and the stones—not just one time but *three* times, until water filled the trench. Elijah then stepped forward and prayed to God, asking Him to demonstrate His power in order to prove He is the one and only living God.

Instantly, the Lord answered Elijah's prayer in a manner every bit as sensational as the challenge itself: "Then the fire of the Lord fell and burned up the sacrifice, the wood, the stones and the soil, and also licked up the water in the trench" (1 Kings 18:38).

Amazing, right? Not only did the sacrifice ignite, but the wood, the stones, the dirt and water burned as well! While the display burned, the people watching proclaimed, "The Lord—he is God!" (verse 39). Elijah then ordered the prophets of Baal to be executed, which apparently sent Ahab and Jezebel past their tipping points. Enraged, the queen sent a messenger to warn Elijah that she would not rest until the prophet had been killed.

But her threats did not change the outcome. This spiritual showdown, with terms agreed upon by those in attendance, ended as an undeniable victory for the one and only Holy God, Lord of heaven and earth! Given ample time the 450 priests of Baal simply could not do what one man of God did in mere seconds: summon divine power to consume the sacrifice with fire. Just to put a fine point on it, Elijah made it as easy as possible for his opponents while making it extra difficult for himself by drenching the altar.

When God's Spirit empowers you for a holy confrontation, the results always glorify God and advance His Kingdom.

When You Feel the Heat

With the mantle of God fueling his faith, Elijah had spoken up. He knew that in those moments when God's reputation is on the line, silence is not an option. Notice that at the outset, when Elijah described the contest, he stated implicitly that the winner would not simply be a powerful "god," but the Lord, the true God. The mantle of holy confrontation speaks to the sovereignty of the one and only true God.

There are things that no one but the one and only true God can do:

Only God can make something out of nothing (see Genesis 1:1).

Only God can make a way where there is no way (see Isaiah 43:19).

Only God can show up and restore things so that at the end of the day it will be as if no damage has been done (see Luke 22:51).

Only God could send His Son, Jesus, to save us from our sins (see John 3:16).

Only God could design us in His own image (see Genesis
  1:27).

Only God could give us the gift of holy sexuality within the
  intimacy of marriage between one man and one woman
  (see 1 Corinthians 7:3).

Only God could reveal the narrow path of truth that leads us
  to heaven (see John 14:6).

As you push the plow, break the ground and sow the seed, you
will receive a mantle that will empower you to declare, *"Only
God!"* When you are in the midst of holy confrontation, you will
usually feel the heat before you see the fire. And that heat is often
uncomfortable. Even the fire itself, the very evidence you begged
God to send to show His power, can be terrifying.

In fact, let me tell you about the fire.

The fire does not primarily make you dance with joy.

The fire first and foremost makes you bow in repentance.

The fire sanctifies you.

The fire purifies you.

The fire refines you.

The fire season is the season in your life when God removes
ideas, thoughts, actions, behavior and even relationships, even
people, from your life that in the future would impede the fulfillment of *His* purpose in you, with you and through you.

Others who walk with the Lord, like modern Obadiahs, will
not be able to do what God has anointed you alone to do. As
others walk alongside you, however, you will begin to realize who
shares your same values and beliefs and who does not. Whom you
can count on—and whom you cannot. Sometimes the fire season
reveals that certain relationships are only for a brief span or a

particular purpose. Then there are times when others are going through the fire whom you may be called to assist.

In our world we see far too many instances of injustice, prejudice, child abuse, hatred, racism—the list goes on. We must be willing to build our altars with stones of righteousness and justice, and trust the hand of God to respond with power. If we remain complacent, then we are complicit. Instead, we must raise our cries as a clarion call for justice and reform, for confession and forgiveness, for healing and restoration.

Having experienced, for instance, the consequences of prejudice firsthand throughout my life, I have learned that change happens only when the mantle of holy confrontation is unfurled. As followers of Jesus, we must do our part by recognizing truth and demonstrating our love in action. Our example must reflect God's love for all people even as it recognizes the travesty, trials and tragedy that the disenfranchised have suffered. We issue our call for change not from a political center but from the prophetic center, where righteousness and justice, grace and truth meet in order to bring peace to all human beings made equally in the image of God.

Together, we survive the droughts and fires and celebrate what comes next—showers of blessings.

Refreshed by Rain

They seem to last forever, those days when the ground is dusty and cracked, and the streams and lakes dry up. When times are hard and we struggle to get by. When we can only imagine standing with faces and hands raised to heaven as rain washes over us. But the drought will end, and the fire, which purifies our desires in the heat of the moment, will fall. And, in time, the fire will burn out, leaving only dying ashes. Then the skies will open and steady curtains of rain will come.

The drought will *reveal* you.

The fire will *refine* you.

The rain will *refresh* you!

Through the drought-enduring, the spiritual-reckoning and the fire-summoning phases—all elements of plow pushing—we trust God to see us through. In hindsight, we glimpse how He prepared and equipped us for the blessings and resources now being entrusted to us. The rain represents holy restoration and renewal, quenching the thirst and abating the hunger experienced during the drought and the fire.

In God's Word, He tells us this: "In the proper season I will send the showers they need. There will be showers of blessing" (Ezekiel 34:26 NLT). As life-giving streams of living water nourish and hydrate us, we realize that God is going to add over here what we lost over there! "The Lord will send rain at the proper time from his rich treasury in the heavens and will bless all the work you do" (Deuteronomy 28:8).

Just like Elijah, you and I will persevere and wear the Christ-centered, grace-tailored mantle that is given only after we survive the drought, pray down fire and thrive in the rain. After the holy fire consumed everything on Elijah's altar, he told Ahab, "Go, eat and drink, for there is the sound of a heavy rain" (1 Kings 18:41). While the king acted on the prophet's words, Elijah "climbed to the top of Mount Carmel, bent down to the ground and put his face between his knees" (verse 42).

After being the conduit for holy confrontation that God used to silence the idolaters, Elijah humbled himself and gave God all the glory. The prophet knew that when you go high you must bow low. The more you experience God's outpouring of power, grace, peace and abundance, the more praise and thanksgiving should flow out of you.

And waiting on the rain requires patience. Elijah told his servant to go and look toward the sea, which he did, only to report no change in the sky. Elijah sent him back seven times before his servant reported, "A cloud as small as a man's hand is rising from the sea" (verse 44).

You, too, must surround yourself with people who will not stop looking for the rain, people who will not stop waiting for the fulfillment of God's promise, who will not grow weary of climbing up mountains. These are the people who can recognize the small beginnings of something powerful, something of God, even from a great distance. Once they tell you they see a small cloud, you take action. And those who prayed with you in the drought and persevered with you in the fire deserve to dance with you in the rain!

Together, we rejoice and praise God for keeping His promises. Once we overcome the obstacles blocking the path, we can bask in the rain of blessings God showers upon us. We can look back at all we survived, endured and pushed to get to the mountaintop. And surely, we have all overcome something in order to reach the summit achieved by holy confrontation.

What did we overcome?

We overcame generational strongholds.

We overcame failure.

We overcame defeat.

We overcame sin.

We overcame temptation.

We overcame addiction.

We overcame depression.

We overcame anxiety.

We overcame confusion.

We overcame infirmity.

We overcame betrayal.

We overcame brokenness.

We overcame unbelief.

We overcame unforgiveness.

We overcame negativity.

We overcame toxic relationships.

We overcame illness.

We overcame the devil.

We overcame others' judgments.

And above all, we overcame ourselves!

Yes, we have overcome so much, and we must never forget all that God has brought us through. But we must also remember *how* we overcame all that is behind us, how we survived the hell we had to face, how we persevered with our plows in order get to our mantles. And let's be honest about our limitations, okay? Because we did not overcome by relying on ourselves and our own power.

No matter how powerful, faithful, brilliant, beautiful, rich, educated or accomplished you may be, you never reach mountain-tops and experience the rain of restoration in your own power.

Not with your tweets.

Not with your selfies.

Not with your political affiliation.

Not with your biology.

Not with your ideology.

You overcame because God fought for you when you could not fight for yourself: "Do not be afraid or discouraged. . . . For the battle is not yours, but God's" (2 Chronicles 20:15).

You overcame because God commanded His angels to surround you: "For the Scriptures say, 'He will order his angels to protect and guard you'" (Luke 4:10 NLT).

You overcame because God stood up for you: "Arise, O LORD, and let your enemies be scattered! Let them flee before you!" (Numbers 10:35 NLT).

You overcame because God gave you authority: "Look, I have given you authority over all the power of the enemy, and you can walk among snakes and scorpions and crush them. Nothing will injure you" (Luke 10:19 NLT).

You overcame because God covered you with His protection: "The LORD will keep you from all evil; he will keep your life. The LORD will keep your going out and your coming in from this time forth and forevermore" (Psalm 121:7–8 ESV).

You overcame because once an overcomer through God's power, always an overcomer through God's power: "We know that everyone who has been born of God does not keep on sinning, but he who was born of God protects him, and the evil one does not touch him" (1 John 5:18).

The enemy came to rob, kill and destroy you (see John 10:10).

Jesus came to give you life, and life abundantly (see John 10:10).

When the rains come, it is time to get back everything the enemy robbed, attempted to kill and tried his best to destroy. Now through the power of Jesus Christ, you are getting it all back.

You are getting your faith back.

You are getting your joy back.

You are getting your peace back.

You are getting your love back.

You are getting your anointing back.

You are getting your dream back.

You are getting your health back.

You are getting your family back.

You are getting your integrity back.

You are getting your character back.

You are getting your reputation back.

You are getting your spiritual hunger back.

You are getting your praise back.

You are getting your shout back.

You are getting your dance back.

You are getting your worship spirit back!

Once you are an overcomer, a survivor and a veteran of pushing plows, then you will trample on everything hell puts in your way. Overcomers survive in order to thrive. They have a testimony that is charged with the power of the living God. Once again, don't simply take my word for it—take the Word of God for it:

> And I heard a loud voice in heaven saying: "Now have come the salvation and the power and the kingdom of our God, and the authority of His Christ. For the accuser of our brothers has been thrown down—he who accuses them day and night before our God. They have conquered him by the blood of the Lamb and by the word of their testimony. And they did not love their lives so as to shy away from death. Therefore rejoice, O heavens, and you who dwell in them!"
>
> Revelation 12:10–12 BSB

Notice here, those who conquered did not just wield the blood of the Lamb—they lifted high the blood of the Lamb *and the word of their testimony*. Christ's blood and your word. Your testimony is a powerful tool in overcoming the enemy. Think about that for just a moment: Your testimony is a conduit for the supernatural, infinite, unlimited power of the Holy Spirit. Your testimony can shift atmospheres. Your testimony can push back darkness.

Look at what the Lord has done in your life:

Look: What the Lord has done silences the devil.

Look: What the Lord has done places Satan underneath your feet.

Look: What the Lord has done disarms principalities and powers of darkness.

You overcame what you went through; that is your testimony. With holy sensitivity, and without giving the enemy any glory for how he tempted and tried to thwart you, use your testimony.

Use your testimony to save others.

Use your testimony to deliver others.

Use your testimony to heal others.

Use your testimony to protect others from what you went through.

God will develop you by using the very thing the enemy sent to destroy you.

Instead of destroying you, it is going to develop you.

Instead of crushing you, it is going to create something new out of you.

Instead of silencing you, it will increase your volume.

Our minds have to catch up to what God's Spirit is doing.

We do not necessarily have to overcome immediately. Sometimes overcoming is a process. And sometimes the overcoming takes place in private so the overflow can take place in public.

But no matter what you are experiencing right now, do not doubt for one second that God is at work in your life. Never be afraid of the battles you face, because the war has already been won. Take your stand for the truth of God's Word and the love He has for all people.

And remember, confrontation requires conviction.

But *holy* confrontation requires the power of God's Spirit.

Push Your Plow, Meet Your Mantle

By this time you know the following questions are provided to help you process and apply the truths shared in this chapter. Similarly, the brief prayer is offered as a way to begin your conversation with God about all you are learning and experiencing in your heart right now.

Try to find some uninterrupted, undistracted time so that you can worship the Lord and listen to the voice of His Spirit in your life. Ask God to show you where you need to take a stand and make the voice of truth heard amidst the clamor.

1. When have you found yourself in a position that required you to take a stand for God's truth? What was at stake? How did you prepare for the holy confrontation you felt led to have? What was the result?

2. What are some of the cultural idols you see others worship and serve in our world today? What impact does their idolatry have on you, your family and your community? How have you confronted these idolaters with the power of God? What was their response?

3. What have you overcome in order to get where you are now in your life? How did you see God at work in helping you remove the obstacles you had to overcome? What mountain might He be calling you to climb next?

Dear God, I know You want me to live in Your truth so that I can be salt and light to the world around me. Too often I am tempted to take the easy way out and just go with the flow rather than take a stand and make my voice heard. Give me the courage of Elijah when he confronted Ahab and the 450 prophets of Baal so that I can summon Your power to overcome idolatry and darkness. Considering all the turmoil in our world today, I need the wisdom and guidance of Your Spirit so that I know how best to achieve peace, reconciliation and healing. Let everything I do be for Your glory and honor, Lord, as I bow on each summit You allow me to climb. Amen.

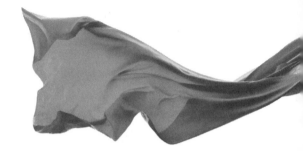

5

The Mantle of Spiritual Momentum

Spiritual momentum allows you to pick up the pace as you trust God more and more—when heaven starts it, hell cannot stop it!

I have loved running for as long as I can remember. Growing up, I quickly realized that I was not the fastest or strongest or most competitive on the track, but I could set a pace and maintain it for more laps than most other runners. Typically, runners either train for speed and compete in dashes and sprints or else focus on endurance and see how fast a pace they can sustain over a longer distance. While I have incorporated training techniques of both over the years, I like to think of myself more as a runner focused on momentum.

Maybe it is because I am also a science geek and love seeing the brilliance of God's design in His creation, but the physics of momentum fascinates me. Here is how it works: When you start running, one foot in front of the other, you begin a rapid succession of push-offs and landings. Simply put, one foot uses the resistance of the ground to spring forward while the other foot in front lands and instantly pushes against the ground for another lift up. As you run forward, the force of your first step is added to your next step, thus creating a faster running speed, step by step and stride by stride.

Momentum in running makes it easier to increase your speed and maintain it, setting a rhythmic pace as your legs and feet work in synchronicity. Without momentum, you would have to exert greater force to keep going at your same rate of motion. Scientifically, the formula for calculating momentum is your body's mass multiplied by the velocity of a desired speed. Hardcore runners—you know, the kind who obsess and keep runner's logs—might calculate their desired momentum by multiplying their weight (usually in kilograms) by their velocity (meters per second).

If we broaden our understanding of momentum beyond running, then we see it is conceptually measured the same way. In physics, momentum is the main quantity that measures the motion of a body, not necessarily the human body but any object or particle within a scientific frame of reference. The law of conservation of momentum indicates that an object's motion will not change over time thanks to its momentum—unless another force intervenes to slow or stop it.

Just consider the way an object that weighs more than another will go farther when both are released at the same speed, assuming any resistance (such as air or water) is the same. If you release a baseball and a bowling ball on a smooth floor at the same speed, the bowling ball will keep going longer (unless it hits a wall or you stop it) than the baseball, which weighs several pounds less.

Or if you roll two bowling balls but alter their velocity, the one going faster will obviously cover a greater distance.

It is simple really: Momentum maximizes movement for forward motion.

The Speed of Life

If you got lost in my geek-speak science lesson, please forgive me. Even if you are not a runner, engineer or physicist, you have some idea of momentum based on personal experience. Simply put, once you get going, it is easier to go faster as you keep going. Momentum describes the way you tend to pick up speed once you are moving forward. Consider how it is typically easier to keep working after finding a kind of self-sustaining pace for doing the tasks your work requires.

You might, for example, be cleaning your home, selling products online or tackling items on someone else's to-do list. Maybe you procrastinate, overwhelmed by all that needs doing and the energy required to do it. Then finally you overcome your inertia and get going. Soon you realize that the more you do, the more you want to keep going and do all that needs to be done. You start slow but pick up speed until you have accomplished the tasks at hand. You refrain from taking a break, stopping to chat with customers or pausing to return a text because you know it will break your high-energy pace. That sense of picking up speed, generally speaking, is your momentum.

Spiritual momentum works much the same way, at least based on my experience and observations. The more we trust God and step out in faith, the stronger our faith in Him the next time we are required to take a risk in moving forward. The more we experience God's power, purpose and peace in our lives, the more we want to experience it all the time. The more we get to know the love, kindness and mercy of the Lord, the more we want everyone to know Him as Lord and Savior.

This kind of pure spiritual momentum could keep us moving forward—in our lives, our relationships, our work, our ministries—in a fairly consistent straight line at a fairly consistent pace. In our fallen world, however, full of every kind of opposition to godly living, spiritual momentum can be difficult to maintain. Instead of growing spiritually at the same pace in the same way no matter what happens day after day, we usually run up against walls that slow or block our progress.

Our circumstances, relationships, decisions, moods, mistakes and triumphs all tend to affect the way we relate to God and rely on His Spirit for our power. Ideally, of course, we should not let our disappointments, failures, regrets and emotions influence our spiritual lives, but since none of us is perfect like Jesus just yet, the reality is that our forward motion is affected by obstacles.

We want to develop a steady, strong spiritual momentum, but then layoffs at work rock our security. A child gets sick and requires hospitalization. The car breaks down and needs a new transmission. Bills begin snowballing into an avalanche of debt. An accident requires a long recovery time, leading to discouragement and impatience. We relapse into old addictions or bad habits or unhealthy relationships.

The many complications of life will almost surely decrease our spiritual momentum—unless we rely on the power of the Holy Spirit. We know that in this life we will always have problems, that the world will always persecute us, and that we will have crosses to bear as we follow the example set by Jesus. But the truth is, the ups and downs of life need not deter us from maintaining our spiritual momentum or regaining it should we lose it.

Through everything we experience, God is there with us. His Spirit is the breath of fresh air that lifts our sails and gives us a second wind. His Son, Jesus, is the Lord for whom we run our races of life. Yes, we may stumble, slow down or slack off, but God is always there to help us get back on our feet and hit our spiritual stride again.

Being determined to persevere, to keep pushing our plows, is the only way we can regain or build our spiritual momentum. If we are to experience the fullness of all God has for us and receive our mantles of promotion, we must trust Him for all our needs and not be distracted, disrupted or disturbed by the interruptions, obstacles and adversaries in our paths. We are sons and daughters of the King, created in our Creator's holy image, co-heirs with Jesus Christ, and immortal beings temporarily in mortal bodies.

Our enemy, the devil, knows that the way to stop us in our spiritual tracks is by tempting, threatening and taunting us. Once we have accepted the free gift of salvation through Jesus' sacrifice on the cross, once we have God's Spirit living within us, then the enemy knows he cannot have us for eternity—but he can still neutralize us. He can undermine our faith, plant seeds of doubt and fear, tempt us to disobey God, and deceive us with lies that distort the truth of God's Word. Once the enemy gets a foothold in our lives, once he gets inside our heads, then he can prevent us from experiencing the abundant life of a joyful purpose for God's Kingdom.

Quite predictably, the enemy often attacks us right after a major spiritual victory.

When we are on our mountaintop praising God, the devil is plotting how to bring us down.

That is certainly what happened to Elijah.

Sore Losers

Elijah had to be enjoying God's victory on Mount Carmel in ways hard to describe. After everything the prophet had experienced at the hands of Ahab and Jezebel, Elijah did not simply wear the mantle of holy confrontation; he had a designer suit made out of it! The confrontation with Baal resulted in clear, unmistakable, unquestionable proof of God's holy existence, singular identity and unlimited power.

In light of this victory, Elijah really had to have enraged his royal adversaries. Talk about sore losers! I am not sure who was angrier and perhaps more humiliated after the sacrificial show-down on Mount Carmel, Ahab or his wicked queen, Jezebel. A strong case can be made for the latter based on the fact that she sent a messenger straight to Elijah with her intentions: "May the gods strike me and even kill me if by this time tomorrow I have not killed you just as you killed them" (1 Kings 19:2 NLT). While her murderous threat is no surprise, you might not expect Elijah to react the way he did in response. Simply put, Elijah panicked!

Rather than stand up to such bullying, Elijah revealed a very human reaction most of us can identify with:

> Elijah was afraid and ran for his life. When he came to Beersheba in Judah, he left his servant there, while he himself went a day's journey into the wilderness. He came to a broom bush, sat down under it and prayed that he might die.
>
> 1 Kings 19:3–4

I cannot recall the first time I heard this story and paid attention, most likely when I was a young teenager. But I do remember being surprised by this bold prophet's sudden case of the jitters! This is the same guy God used to stop all rain for nearly three years? The same man who camped out in the ravine beside the brook, where ravens fed him? The prophet of the Lord who miraculously proclaimed the widow's flour and oil would not run out? Who raised her son from the dead?

The same Elijah who obeyed God through a holy confrontation with the king and queen, their pagan prophets and the apostate people of Israel? The victor in a showdown that not only showed God's power as compared to the impotence of Baal, but proved God's identity as the one and only true God?

The same person who did all that suddenly felt afraid and ran away by himself into the wilderness, where he was so despondent he wanted to die?

Yep. It is the same person. And before you or I judge Elijah too harshly as a coward, we might want to take a look at the logs in our own eyes first. Walking by faith means that we want to rely on God all the time, trusting Him to lead, guide, protect and provide for us. But wanting to rely on God all the time does not make us immune to devastating losses, horrendous disappointments and overwhelming emotions.

When he allowed fear to enter his heart and Jezebel to get in his head, Elijah also allowed his spiritual momentum to be jolted abruptly into a series of stops and starts based on his emotions. He went from being the conductor of a heavenly bullet train to being held hostage on a roller coaster of feelings suddenly screeching to a halt! Looking back at the full narrative of his life, we struggle to make sense of what exactly went wrong.

But we might ask ourselves the same question.

You can probably look at your life and see some incredible high points when God intervened in amazing, generous, miraculous ways that you still celebrate to this day. You can likely also see moments when you so disappointed yourself by the way you turned away from God that it still stirs up feelings of shame inside you. These mile markers remind us that our spiritual momentum often follows a stop-and-start-again pace then a blistering speed of constant advancement.

The important thing is to get moving again.

To remember who you really are, Who made you, and what you are called to do.

Where you are right now and where you are going for eternity.

When you are going at a fast speed and then suddenly hit a wall or have someone run into you, you are going to be disoriented. But as you get back on your feet and regain your bearings, you can refocus on what you know is true.

Because how can you stay down when the same Spirit who raised Jesus from the dead lives inside of you? When you rely on God to sustain you, then you always have the power necessary to keep going. And in order to avoid those sudden stops and derailments, it is important to look where you are going.

Are you following God and the path revealed by His Spirit?

Or someone or something else?

Sticky Traps

In order to wear the mantle of spiritual momentum we have to determine whom we serve. There are people who flatter their way into influencing us just as there are people who provoke us because they want our attention or who criticize us in a way that gets under our skin.

These people know that a distraction is the first step to a disruption, and they enjoy the feeling of power this gives them.

Tell your story for God's glory, not for your own or for anyone else's approval. Tell your story in the mountaintop moments when you have seen God work in amazing and miraculous ways in your life. Tell your story when the Lord has sustained you through the drought and delivered the holy fire to defeat your enemies and refine the impurities in your life.

Tell your story to those willing to listen and acknowledge God's power and presence in your life. If they join you in worshiping Him as the one and only true God, then you have discovered new friends in the Body of Christ. That is the only way people can have any authority or credibility to speak into your life—if they are walking with God and serving Him as their Lord and Savior.

More often, those without the spiritual authority to influence you will try to tell you what you should and should not do. These may be family and friends, but they may also be online influencers, cultural icons, celebrities, actors, singers, performers, superstar athletes, politicians or civic leaders—and, yes, sometimes even those who claim falsely to be believers, pastors and ministry leaders! Jesus warned us about these wolves in sheep's clothing:

> "Not everyone who says to me, 'Lord, Lord,' will enter the kingdom of heaven, but only the one who does the will of my Father who is in heaven. Many will say to me on that day, 'Lord, Lord, did we not prophesy in your name and in your name drive out demons and in your name perform many miracles?' Then I will tell them plainly, 'I never knew you. Away from me, you evildoers!'"
>
> Matthew 7:21–23

These evildoers will attempt the same thing Jezebel did: to start a conversation with you, to engage you in ways that give them a foothold for influence. Why else would Jezebel send a message worded in such a way, if not to plant seeds of doubt, fear and uncertainty in Elijah's mind? If she really wanted to kill Elijah, might she not have sent a soldier rather than a messenger? Instead, she sent a time bomb with great potential for prolonging Elijah's fearful, worst-case imaginings: "May the gods strike me and even kill me," she said, "if by this time tomorrow I have not killed you just as you killed the prophets of Baal."

Notice the three ways she tried to penetrate Elijah's spiritual, emotional and physical defenses here. First, she invoked her own gods against herself—making it clear that she still did not believe in the one true living God. By asking her gods to strike her dead if she failed to honor her death threat, Jezebel used counterintuitive logic. Elijah already knew her gods were false idols without the power to generate a spark let alone a fire. She could make oaths to them all she wanted without causing him any fear. But the fact that she was willing to invoke them implied that she thought her gods *did* have that kind of power. Evil loves to create doubts that lead to sticky traps!

Next, moving from spiritual to emotional tactics, Jezebel conveyed to Elijah that she was out for revenge, planning to kill him just as he had had all 450 prophets of Baal killed. She intended to spark fear in this mighty man of God and hoped to impress to Elijah by her passionate fury. Finally, Jezebel set a deadline—"by this time tomorrow"—in order to intensify Elijah's anxiety and uncertainty. Setting this 24-hour window in place made her intent sound deliberate; this was not a vague threat.

Jezebel wanted a conversation, and based on Elijah's reaction, she got one.

Do not converse with Jezebels in your life. *Rebuke* Jezebels.

This is a method the crafty enemy employed way back in the Garden of Eden, asking Eve, "Did God really say, 'You must not eat from any tree in the garden'?" (Genesis 3:1). The serpent, who knew the answer to his own question before he asked it, exaggerated the instruction God had given his male and female creations by taking it to the extreme. But the serpent's question had done what it was intended to do—start a conversation.

After Eve corrected the serpent's implied assumption about what she and Adam could and could not eat, the serpent pulled his next trick of temptation by trying to undermine God's authority: "'You will certainly not die,' the serpent said to the woman. 'For God knows that when you eat from it your eyes will be opened, and you will be like God, knowing good and evil'" (Genesis 3:4–5).

She was caught in the verbal trap. She ate, and Adam, who was there with her, ate.

Enemies know how to engage us, and once we are engaged, then we can be distracted, divided, diverted and derailed from our God-given purpose. Once we are off-track, then our own emotions do much of the work. As we begin letting our imaginations wander, our worst fears come to mind, old memories of similar feelings are triggered, and we begin to feel helpless, cutting off our reliance on God and the power of the Holy Spirit usually without even realizing it.

But when we move under the mantle of spiritual momentum, our enemies cannot stop us. They might slow us down, throw us down or mow us down, but they cannot stop us.

They can try to threaten us so that we come to a temporary halt. *But once God sets us in motion, we are unstoppable!*

Been There and Done That

Elijah let his fear get the best of him. After all that he had experienced, after all he had seen God do, after all that he had witnessed, Elijah ran away to hide. He let his trust in the Lord slip away and overlooked the truth of God's Word: "Do not be afraid or discouraged, for the LORD will personally go ahead of you. He will be with you; he will neither fail you nor abandon you" (Deuteronomy 31:8 NLT).

What does this mean? Why is this promise so important? Because it gives us fuel for the engine of spiritual momentum. We can keep pressing forward with certainty no matter who or what tries to stop us. Even as Elijah ran to Beersheba, where he left his servant behind and then hid alone under the broom tree, God was already there.

It means that no matter what lies before you, when you move toward it, God is already there. He paved your path of promotion before you ever took your first step. So no matter what obstacle, barrier, impediment, roadblock, speed bump or pothole you hit, God has already gone ahead of you and provided a way forward.

That river that is in front of you: God has already crossed it.

That mountain that stands in your way: God has already climbed it.

That viper that came out to poison you: God has already shaken it off.

That giant who mocks and threatens you: God has already knocked him down.

That Jezebel who is making threats to destroy you: God has already silenced her.

God always goes ahead and prepares the way for you to do greater things.

All you must do is keep moving, keep trusting, keep going—keep plowing.

God's Word confirms this: "I tell you the truth, anyone who believes in me will do the same works I have done, and even greater works, because I am going to be with the Father" (John 14:12 NLT).

God goes ahead of you.

God is for you and not against you.

No matter what you are facing, God has already solved it, fixed it, resolved it, removed it, healed it and sealed it. If you are concerned about your children, your family, your marriage, that medical report, your career, your education, that relationship, that circumstance, that wound from the past, that scar of betrayal, that secret keeping you awake at night, that addiction you are still battling, then here is what you must know: *Let not your heart be troubled.*

Do not worry.

Do not be anxious.

Why? Because God has already dealt with it. He has been there and done that.

"But, Pastor Sam, you don't understand what I'm up against. This year has been so hard, so painful, so scary—I don't know how I can keep going. I don't know how anyone can keep going in light of what I'm facing."

God knows. And He is ahead of you working on your behalf.

He is preparing the way, clearing the path, fighting the battles, exposing the traps, mining the diamonds, all because He loves you.

Go at God's Speed

If you are still reluctant to believe this promise from God's Word, then remember Elijah. I suspect he felt all the emotions you are feeling and thought many of the same desperate thoughts. He was someone who walked with God, trusted God and knew the power of God, but yet Elijah struggled in his faith. When we consider the big picture of Elijah's life, however, and we see his mantle of spiritual momentum, then we can see God's hand on him.

Jezebel swore by her gods that Elijah would die in 24 hours. But then 24 hours came and went, and Elijah did not die. Then

48 hours passed, and 72 hours went by, and 96 hours, and now more than 2,800 years later, Elijah has yet to die!

What do I mean by that? Jezebel claimed that she would kill Elijah or die trying, but guess what? Elijah lived long after Jezebel had made her last threat or worshiped her last idol. And eventually, how did Elijah die? *He didn't!* "As they were walking along and talking, suddenly a chariot of fire appeared, drawn by horses of fire. It drove between [him and Elisha], separating them, and Elijah was carried by a whirlwind into heaven" (2 Kings 2:11 NLT).

Can you believe this? Not only was Elijah not killed by Jezebel—he did not die at all. And not only did he not die, but guess who appeared on the Mount of Transfiguration with Jesus centuries later? Elijah. Not only did he not die, but Elijah appeared with Jesus in the high place (see Matthew 17:2–3).

So let's hit pause for just a moment and go back to what is weighing on you and slowing you down. No matter how heavy it feels or overwhelming it appears, I am here to tell you that whatever Jezebel declared upon you and your family will never come to pass. In fact, God has gone before you and just the opposite will take place.

Whatever hell declared upon your health, the opposite will take place.

Whatever the forces of darkness declared upon your ministry, the opposite will take place.

Whatever the enemy declared to stop your momentum, God will use to empower you even more.

Here on earth, Newton's Third Law of Motion, from which the law of conservation of momentum was derived, tells us that "for every action, there is an equal and opposite reaction." But let me tell you God's Promise of Spiritual Motion: "For every threat, attempt, temptation or snare made by the enemy, God will not only provide a way forward, He will bless you for trusting Him and persevering."

Which means what exactly? It means you are not stopping; you are just getting started.

It means it is not too late; it is time to keep going.

It means you are not going to die; you are going to live.

You are not going down; you are going up.

You are not going to fail; you are going to thrive.

Your family will not be lost; your family will be saved.

The enemy will not take this generation—this generation will usher in the greatest spiritual awakening we have ever seen.

Why? Because when heaven starts it, hell cannot stop it.

Let me speak metaphorically with 21st-century contextualization: How many times has hell posted a photo of you looking defeated on its Instagram account only to have to delete it because of a case of mistaken identity? When has your memory been temporarily deleted only to discover you have divine backup? How has God rebooted your life when the enemy infected you with a virus?

If you are wondering why you are still here, then realize that what you carry is greater than what you go through. What God has placed *in* you is greater than what the devil has placed in front of you. The mantle of spiritual momentum that the Lord has placed on you will carry you up, over, around and through whatever hurdles the enemy uses to slow you down. You are going at God's speed, not the speed of life.

What the enemy sent to destroy you, God will use to develop you.

The enemy has a destructive plan; God will turn it around into His development project.

You are here because the blood upon you is greater than the battle in front of you.

You are here because you and your family are covered by the blood of Jesus.

You are here . . . because you overcame Jezebel!

And you overcame Jezebel . . .

Not by your strength.

Not by your bank account.

Not by your political affiliation.

Not by your theology.

Not by your personality.

Not by your gifting.

Not by your social media presence.

Not by your postings.

Not by your tweets.

Not by your selfies.

And not by your mental intelligence, emotional intelligence or military intelligence

You overcame by the blood of the Lamb and the word of your testimony (see Revelation 12:11). That is right. You have something Elijah did not have: You are covered by the blood of the Lamb, Jesus Christ, God's only Son who died on the cross to pay the price for your sins once and for all. If Elijah made it through without the blood, imagine how far you will make it!

I dare you to confront your Jezebel and say, "You can't break through the blood of the Lamb."

I dare you to look at your Ahab and say, "You can't break through the blood of the Lamb."

I dare you to look at Baal and your other idols and say, "You can't break through the blood of the Lamb of God."

Get ready to prove the devil wrong.

Get ready to make Jezebel a liar.

Your testimony is proof that the devil is a liar.

You are covered by the blood shed by Jesus Christ on the cross of Calvary. Your spiritual momentum relies on what He has already done, what He is doing, and what He will do in your life. Your journey is fueled by God's Word and driven by the engine of His Holy Spirit.

His blood is upon you.

His Spirit is inside of you.

His Word goes before you.

Goodness and mercy and signs and wonders follow you.

Why are you here right now? How did you get to this point in your life? What did God do when He went ahead of you to make a way so you could be right here, right now, reading these words before your very eyes?

Because you have something more than the mantle of spiritual momentum—*you have the Mantle Maker.*

Jezebel has missed her chance. Hell has lost its opportunity. The devil has slipped because you are keeping your hand to the plow. You are giving the devil no conversation. God has given you tools to overcome the enemy without ever slowing down.

Your prayer will stop your enemy.

Your praise of God will confuse your enemy.

Your peace will paralyze him.

Your integrity will disarm him.

And your resistance will make him flee.

You have the mantle of God on your shoulders so do not be afraid to use it.

God has set the pace for your spiritual momentum. All you have to do is keep walking by faith each day, step by step, stride by stride.

So let nothing slow you down, my friend.

Godspeed!

Push Your Plow, Meet Your Mantle

Runners know that they need to stay nourished and hydrated in order to maintain their energy levels, speed and momentum. Followers of Jesus also need sustenance in order to run the race of faith at a steady pace of strong spiritual momentum. This is why it is so important to read and study God's Word, to pray and spend time alone with the Lord, to worship and praise Him, to serve and have fellowship with other believers. In order to grow in our faith, we all need life-giving nutrients of truth, love, peace and joy.

Use the following questions as a way of taking a quick pit stop for spiritual refreshment. After taking a few minutes to answer them, and perhaps write down your answers, spend some time silently in prayer. Think about how far God has brought you and where you see Him leading you next. Thank Him for what He has done and how He has provided for you, and express your trust in Him to help you keep going.

1. Think of a time when you experienced physical momentum in your everyday life. When did you start a project or pursue a goal and gain momentum as you got more and more done?

2. Have you experienced an increase of spiritual momentum in your life? What contributed to that season of growth, closeness to God and maturity? How did you see God at work during that time? How did your awareness of His presence and power in your life motivate you to keep going?

3. What barriers have you faced recently that have slowed you down spiritually? How did they make you feel? How is God's Spirit giving you a second wind to keep going right now?

Dear Lord, I am so grateful for the ways You guide and direct my paths. I praise You and give You thanks for the gift of Your Holy Spirit within me! Help me to follow Your Spirit's lead, not lagging behind and not running ahead, so that I am going at Your holy and perfect pace and not my own. Remind me that I am an overcomer and that I need not slow down when Jezebels make empty threats or I feel afraid. Give me Your peace that passes understanding and the power of Your Spirit so that I can keep walking in the footsteps of Jesus each and every day. Amen.

6

Tuck and Run

We are often waiting for God to answer our prayers while God is waiting for us to be ready for His answer—His prophetic power always exceeds our pathetic times!

Certain irrational forces demanding my fanatic devotion began pressuring me at a young age. These powerful groups were often clad in black-and-gold or green-and-silver, with a variety of numbers and names adorning their garments. No, it was not a denominational tug-of-war or spiritual warfare—at least, I don't think it was.

My struggle was simply the result of growing up in Bethlehem, Pennsylvania, during the '70s and early '80s, where one's favorite sports teams were geographically predetermined. But it was not always that simple: Economic and social factors also weighed heavily on our choices.

The dichotomy was clear. For Pennsylvanians, the professional sports teams were based out of either Pittsburgh, the Steel City in the western corner of the state, or Philadelphia, the historic City of Brotherly Love in the eastern corner. Pittsburgh had the Steelers, a legendary National Football League dynasty with multiple Super Bowl wins, along with the Major League Baseball Pirates, and the National Hockey League Penguins. Pittsburgh fans, particularly those devoted to the Steelers, tended to reflect more of a working-class, average-family kind of demographic.

Philadelphia, on the other hand, had more teams—in football the Eagles, in baseball the Phillies, in hockey the Flyers and, in the National Basketball Association, the 76ers—and a broader, more urban, East Coast appeal. I grew up about sixty miles north of Philly, which meant I should root for her teams. My town, Bethlehem, however, had been the second largest steel producer in our country for several decades, which means it had more in common with the city most frequently in first place for steel production, Pittsburgh.

As a Rust Belt city, Bethlehem also attracted a large immigrant population of factory and steel mill workers. People from Poland, Slovakia, Ukraine and Italy were prevalent along with an assortment from other international locales. My family had emigrated from Puerto Rico and settled in Bethlehem because my father found work on a Mack truck assembly line. All to say, I grew up in a community with more of a Pittsburgh attitude while being only an hour away from historic Philadelphia.

Once I was old enough to begin deciding for myself, I gravitated toward enjoying one Pennsylvania-based NFL team more than the other—but for a reason I am guessing most fans rarely consider as their deciding criterion. (I shall not disclose which team in hopes of preventing angry texts and tweets from fans of the other team, some of whom are related to me!) My favorite team selection resulted from the quarterback's play calling.

While that seems a good enough reason for many football fans, it was not the QB's brilliant strategy or ability to read the opposing team's defense and change the play at the last minute that drew my attention. It was the idiosyncratic, indecipherable, imaginative string of numbers, names and nonsense assembled for any given play, which ended up sounding something like this: "Ohio—42!—16!—Blue—84!—New York!—Hamburger!—Hamburger!" If you have played or watched much football, then you know what I am talking about. The quarterback's goal is to disguise the play, confuse the opponent's defense and be heard at the line of scrimmage. His own team members know which words or numbers signal the actual play being set, and the rest is merely a string of red herrings.

One thing I eventually realized about my favorite quarterback's urgent, nonsensical shouts is that the lengthier and more complex his call, usually the simpler the play. A quick handoff to the running back up the middle might sound like the Gettysburg Address! A short-yardage pass from the pocket could be gibberish mixed into a fast-food drive-through order.

Granted, I am probably one of a small number of fans who came to enjoy the creative calling of plays as much as or more than the actual plays themselves. But once I became a believer, I saw a striking similarity: Often our instructions from God may not make sense in the moment to those around us, but as we obediently carry out those directions our enemy is thwarted and God's Kingdom advanced. God's words to us may not seem logical or rational to others, but His followers who have been anointed know that they will further His will in their lives.

This was certainly the case with Elijah after the big sacrificial showdown.

After more than three years of drought, the rain promised by God was about to begin.

Elijah instructed Ahab to return home to Jezreel, and then ran ahead of the king's chariot.

And in order to win this race, Elijah had to tuck and run.

Rain Delay

You will recall that after the ignite-the-sacrifice contest between the prophets of Baal and Elijah, the results were more than clear. While the idol worshipers spent the better part of the day praying without seeing the first spark, Elijah prayed and holy fire rained down from heaven immediately and consumed everything, including water and dirt, near the sacrifice and altar. The contrast could not have been sharper.

Next, Elijah had the prophets killed and told King Ahab that after the terrible drought, God was about to send rain. Elijah told the king to eat and drink while the prophet went to the top of Mount Carmel, where he bowed before the Lord and prayed. With no time to catch his breath after the miraculous, fiery display of God's power and presence, Elijah prepared for the next miracle, the long-awaited rain to restore the land and its people:

> "Go and look toward the sea," he told his servant. And he went up and looked.
>
> "There is nothing there," he said.
>
> Seven times Elijah said, "Go back."
>
> The seventh time the servant reported, "A cloud as small as a man's hand is rising from the sea."
>
> So Elijah said, "Go and tell Ahab, 'Hitch up your chariot and go down before the rain stops you.'"
>
> Meanwhile, the sky grew black with clouds, the wind rose, a heavy rain started falling and Ahab rode off to Jezreel. The power

of the Lord came on Elijah and, tucking his cloak into his belt, he ran ahead of Ahab all the way to Jezreel.

1 Kings 18:43–46

As is often the case with Scripture, we find many layers packed into a relatively short passage. One of the first aspects of this story to stand out is the rain delay—or at least a delay from an earthly perspective. Surely after God had instantly answered Elijah's prayer and had sent a blaze to consume the altar, the bull, the moat dug around the altar and almost a dozen jugs of water that had dowsed the whole display, it was reasonable to expect the Lord to produce the much-needed rain the same way.

The Lord was more than capable, Elijah had come to recognize, of working in the blink of an eye. After the scorching response just a little while earlier, Elijah might have done the same thing you or I would have likely done and assumed that this next phase would work the same way. After all, Elijah had already told Ahab, "Go, eat and drink, for there is the sound of a heavy rain" (verse 41). Notice there is no qualification, caveat or hedging about when and where the rain would be arriving. Apparently, Elijah could already hear it—if not literally then spiritually because of his implicit faith in God's promise and power.

This level of certainty seems logical enough, again, after what had just happened. Otherwise, it might be more accurate or helpful to tell the king, "God has promised to send rain now, so it should be here in His divine timing." But that is not what Elijah did, even though his confidence in the Almighty was presumably at an all-time high point.

Which only spotlights the scene that followed. Because the downpour did not start right in that moment. Instead, Elijah went and prayed on the mountaintop and sent his servant to check the weather. Not once, not twice, but *seven* times, Elijah sent his servant back to look toward the sea for any sign of rain. Any sign—not a huge stormfront or cloudburst but any indication whatsoever. And the fact that he had to keep sending the servant back again and again must have left the servant wondering what was going on. He, too, had seen what God had performed through his master, Elijah, but then each time the servant went to the vantage point and looked toward the sea, nothing. The skies were blue and clear. No sign of rain whatsoever.

Until finally, *finally*, on that seventh return, the servant caught sight of something: "A cloud as small as a man's hand is rising from the sea." Not exactly the swirling mass of dark rain clouds he was probably looking for. He reported it faithfully to Elijah, however, who saw this tiny cloud as more than enough. More than enough to start the downpour he had asked God to send, more than enough to sprinkle the first few drops of water on the land in three-plus years, more than enough to warn the king to start home before his chariot ended up getting stuck in the mud.

Notice that Elijah did not verify what his servant told him but accepted his report as accurate. His trust reminds us to surround ourselves with people willing to go look for rain clouds again and again. People we can rely on who share our commitment to serving God. People we never doubt when they provide information. People who know that a tiny cloud is worth reporting.

Despite seeing how dramatically God could reveal Himself in His miracles, Elijah had also witnessed the way the Lord often uses just a little to make a lot. He had seen it near the brook of Cherith when the ravens brought just enough food for the prophet each day, not too much and not too little, but just the right amount. He had seen it with the widow he met in Sidon, a woman of faith who was down to her last dab of oil and last sprinkle of flour—but again, just enough, to produce bread for herself, her son and her new guest day after day after day. So when Elijah heard from his servant that a cloud the size of a man's hand had been spotted, the prophet knew this little wisp was more than enough for God to send gale-force winds and a torrential downpour.

And indeed it was! Because "soon the sky was black with clouds" followed by a "heavy wind [that] brought a terrific rainstorm" (1 Kings 18:45 NLT). From the tiny cloud spotted by a servant to a fearsome front that sent the king scrambling into his chariot to get home, God once again kept His promise according to His perfect will and wisdom. Notice the contrast, too, between Elijah—who said he could hear the rain coming long before it did—and Ahab, who did not bother preparing until the storm let loose.

Then in an apparent domino-like sequence of miracles we find one more. After Ahab left in his chariot for Jezreel, God did something else astonishing: "The power of the LORD came on Elijah and, tucking his cloak into his belt, he ran ahead of Ahab all the way to Jezreel" (verse 46).

When Less Is More

I find this almost understated miracle one of the most intriguing in Elijah's entire story. As a runner myself, I am astonished to consider a human being outrunning a horse-drawn chariot. Biblical scholars and historians tell us that most chariots in the Middle East during ancient times were driven by at least two horses. And even though the king's horses were pulling the chariot itself with probably at least two occupants, Ahab and his royal driver, they were certainly strong, fast beasts used to galloping at a quick pace—especially in this instance with the king trying to outrun the rain.

But these majestic stallions were no match for the supernaturally speedy prophet whom God had empowered! Can you just imagine Ahab riding along, eager to get home out of the storm, perhaps wondering why he had not left sooner, when suddenly he saw a man go racing past his royal chariot? Surely, a man could not be running that fast, Ahab must have thought, and then after doing a double take, the king would have realized that it was not only a man running faster than his chariot—it was Elijah, whom he had left back at Mount Carmel!

No matter how physically fit this prophet of God was, such a feat required divine strength, stamina and support, which the power of the Lord provided. Winning such an extraordinary race, however, also required Elijah's complete cooperation. He knew that he could not run the race set before him until he tucked his cloak into his belt.

Left untucked, his loose-fitting garment would entangle his legs. It would be like trying to run a marathon at your fastest, personal-best pace in a floor-length bathrobe. Obviously, most serious runners try to wear as little as possible so that there is nothing to limit their full range of motion. The less clothing, the less weight and the less friction.

In Elijah's day running was a regular means of transportation, not a popular way of keeping fit. His preparation was probably as much a matter of common sense as well as anticipation for what God was doing. Curiously enough, the prophet's tuck before take-off provides an illustration of the metaphoric admonition given centuries later by the apostle Paul: "Therefore, since we are surrounded by such a great cloud of witnesses, let us throw off everything that hinders and the sin that so easily entangles. And let us run with perseverance the race marked out for us" (Hebrews 12:1).

The examples of Elijah and Paul still apply to us today.

When God speaks His directives and empowers us to do the impossible, we must do our part to obey. We do not have to decipher coded messages like football players at the line of scrimmage. We simply have to still our hearts before God, listen for the whisper of the Spirit's voice and do what He asks us to do.

Tuck Now So You Will Not Trip Later

Although sharing this truth from different times and contexts, Elijah and Paul both remind us to run the race of faith with as little friction as possible. While Elijah's is literal and Paul's is symbolic, the lesson remains surprisingly relevant for followers of Jesus in our world today. The prophet tucked his cloak into his belt before putting one foot in front of the other and experiencing physical momentum to match the spiritual momentum already set in motion. Elijah knew better than to start out, even though the Lord had empowered him, without first doing what had to be done to avoid tripping, stumbling and falling.

Many people trip on their own cloaks after they receive their mantles of promotion. They do the hard work God has set before them, pushing their plows faithfully and obediently as they persevere, and they receive the blessings of more resources to steward. But then, humbled and excited, they feel both overwhelmed and unstoppable as they begin moving toward the next level the Lord has for them. To make matters worse, they assume confidence and take credit for what He has done through them. And then suddenly, they trip and fall, having failed to prepare mentally, emotionally and physically in order to handle the new gifts God has poured into them.

Or, in the other usual scenario, when God does not answer them or grant their petitions immediately, they come to a halt, assuming they must wait on God's timing, when actually He is waiting on them to be mature enough to tuck their mantles and run!

I have seen a number of people stumble over their own anointing—and I have come close to stumbling myself at various times. In fact, I am convinced this is the reason why we often make requests and find our prayers going unanswered. We serve diligently and then experience God's blessing as He gives us His mantle of promotion. But when our expectations are not met, we grow impatient and feel confused and disappointed. When what we assume will happen next does *not* happen next, we either barge ahead to make it happen or else fear to move, worrying that we have somehow misunderstood or taken a wrong step. In both cases, we focus on ourselves rather than our willingness to trust God completely and wholeheartedly.

He wants us to be able to handle what we are asking for before giving it to us. God is waiting for us to grow up and demonstrate that we can handle the anointing we think we are ready to experience.

The Lord is waiting for us to exhibit the maturity, wherewithal, fortitude and acumen required to manage the gifts He wants us to have.

And how do we know we are maturing spiritually? Paul said that he knew he was maturing in Christ when the things that used to bother him no longer troubled him. Circumstances, situations and accusations that once caused discomfort and suffering eventually became reasons for Paul to boast about God's strength and power in the midst of his own weaknesses. He explained:

Five times I received from the Jews the forty lashes minus one. Three times I was beaten with rods, once I was pelted with stones, three times I was shipwrecked, I spent a night and a day in the open sea, I have been constantly on the move. I have been in danger from rivers, in danger from bandits, in danger from my fellow Jews, in danger from Gentiles; in danger in the city, in danger in the country, in danger at sea; and in danger from false believers. I have labored and toiled and have often gone without sleep; I have known hunger and thirst and have often gone without food; I have been cold and naked. Besides everything else, I face daily the pressure of my concern for all the churches. Who is weak, and I do not feel weak? Who is led into sin, and I do not inwardly burn?

If I must boast, I will boast of the things that show my weakness.

2 Corinthians 11:24–30

The same standard for assessing spiritual maturity applies to you and me. When the things that used to get on your nerves no longer get on your nerves, then you are maturing. When the people who were once able to stop you from pursuing your destiny with one little word lose their power to hold you back, then you are maturing. When the fleshly desires that once led you into sinful situations no longer have the ability to make you fall, then you are maturing. When you are able to say no to the temptations you used to give in to, then you are maturing.

When you are willing to tuck your mantle, the one you worked so hard to be worthy to receive, the one you plowed with perseverance in order to attain, then you are truly willing to be used by God. Too often, we allow the positions, ministries, churches, titles, accomplishments and resources provided by God to define us. In our desire to reorient ourselves to the new responsibilities that come with our mantles, we often wear them as status symbols, badges of holy honor for others to see, spiritual fashion accessories displaying our status and stature.

Your mantle of promotion is none of those things. It does not accord you a special standing with God—it reflects what is already in place. Keep in mind that Elijah's mantle was not just a cloak, something that could be discarded, lost or ignored. No, his mantle was a symbol of prophetic power, a visual and tactile textile testifying to God's presence and power in Elijah's life. Notice the significant role his mantle played when Elijah passed on his prophetic authority to his successor, Elisha:

> Then Elijah folded his cloak together and struck the water with it. The river divided, and the two of them went across on dry ground!
>
> When they came to the other side, Elijah said to Elisha, "Tell me what I can do for you before I am taken away."
>
> And Elisha replied, "Please let me inherit a double share of your spirit and become your successor."
>
> "You have asked a difficult thing," Elijah replied. "If you see me when I am taken from you, then you will get your request. But if not, then you won't."
>
> As they were walking along and talking, suddenly a chariot of fire appeared, drawn by horses of fire. It drove between the two men, separating them, and Elijah was carried by a whirlwind into heaven. Elisha saw it and cried out, "My father! My father! I see the chariots and charioteers of Israel!" And as they disappeared from sight, Elisha tore his clothes in distress.
>
> Elisha picked up Elijah's cloak, which had fallen when he was taken up. Then Elisha returned to the bank of the Jordan River. He struck the water with Elijah's cloak and cried out, "Where is the LORD, the God of Elijah?" Then the river divided, and Elisha went across.
>
> 2 Kings 2:8–14 NLT

Notice how Elijah protected the mantle representing his anointing for the next generation. He left it behind so that his protégé, Elisha, could pick it up and assume the symbolic authority it carried. So that day when Elijah tucked his cloak into his belt before running to beat Ahab to Jezreel, he was not only focused on traveling unencumbered—Elijah was protecting his mantle for the next generation.

When you wear the mantle of God's promotion in your own life, you too must realize that you are stewarding its prophetic authority for those who will follow behind you. It is not just a matter of what is necessary or comfortable for you in the moment as you complete the mission or run the specific race. It is stewardship of what God is doing for those who inherit your mantle. Never leave your mantle behind as you start your race—you have plowed too hard and waited too long. Instead, tuck it into your belt and start running!

Late Starts Finish First

Even when you have seen the Lord do unbelievable, amazing, incredible, miraculous displays of His power, provision and purpose in your life, you may still be tempted to make excuses that prevent you from experiencing all He has for you. Even when your anointing has facilitated miracles in the lives of others, you may still balk when the next opportunity occurs. Even when you are dedicated and committed in all areas of your life to serving God, you may still feel weary, shaken and uncertain that you have heard correctly His next mission for your life.

One of the biggest excuses when you are up against adversaries that are better equipped, better resourced and better prepared is that it is too late. Maybe you have an idea for a new ministry, and then you see others doing it with more funding, more attention and more success. But if God calls you to do something, none of that matters! Maybe you are trying to begin a new friendship, only you keep comparing yourself to others and coming up short. Maybe a physical disease or injury has left you weak and uncertain whether or not you can ever recover the strength and health you have lost.

Rather than trust God and receive His power, you say, "It's too late. I know nothing is impossible for you, Lord, but I just can't do this. I'm too sick, too afraid, too vulnerable, too weary." Or you might be relying on God and sensing His power, but you are unwilling to tuck and run. You set yourself up for failure by letting your mantle get in the way. You allow your anointing to be more important than the One who anointed you in the first place.

I do not know if any of these thoughts or excuses flashed through Elijah's mind as the rain clouds moved in and began to release a mighty flood from the heavens. But I do know that this man did what God had positioned him to do. He received the divine power God placed on him, and then he tucked his cloak and started running. Elijah did not allow his late start to get in the way of finishing first.

Yes, Ahab left before he did.

Yes, Ahab was possibly miles ahead of him.

Yes, Ahab was on his way to the finish line first.

Yes, Ahab was in a chariot drawn by horses while he was on foot.

Yes, Ahab was bound to win based on logic, probability and common sense.

But you know what?

All those earthly yeses are no match for one heavenly anointing!

God chose this opportunity to remind us all that His ways are not our ways. No matter what kind of technology, machinery, appliances, conveniences or innovations we are using, they can never match the sheer power of the Lord poured over our lives.

In addition to his late start, Elijah also faced the daunting distance from Mount Carmel to Jezreel, roughly fifty kilometers or about thirty miles. Just for perspective, you should know runners today compete in marathons with the standard distance of 26.2 miles. The origin of the marathon as a distance-running event has roots in the story, which may be more fiction than fact, of Pheidippides, a Greek soldier charged with running from his army's battlefield near the town of Marathon to Athens, a distance of approximately 25 miles, in order to deliver the important message that the Persians had been defeated. According to the story, he ran without stopping all the way from Marathon to Athens and upon arrival proclaimed, "Victory!" before collapsing and dying.

So historically, marathons began as 25-mile commemorations of Pheidippides' courageous journey. The extra mile and 385 yards were added later, around the turn of the twentieth century, in response to better-viewing requests by royalty. Considering that Elijah's race with Ahab to the royal residence was likely around five miles longer, maybe we should be running "jezreels" instead of marathons!

The late start did not prevent Elijah from tucking and running.

The length of the course did not stop Elijah from doing what others had likely never done.

The weather conditions, terrain and lack of running shoes did not keep Elijah from running the race God empowered him to run.

While Ahab had horsepower, Elijah had an angelic engine!

Carefree and Careful

My friend, when God empowers you with His call, it is never too late to tuck and run no matter how long the course before you extends. The pathetic may start before you, but the prophetic will always win. The darkness may get a head start, but the light will always finish first. Hell may seem to be in the lead, but heaven will always close the gap and win the race every time.

You may think your creditors will win the battle for your financial solvency, but God's power will provide and meet your needs. Cancer may have started first, but your prayers will unleash God's healing so that your health wins the race. You might assume those who have betrayed you at work have won the promotion, but God does not play office favorites. He empowers and blesses those who hear Him, believe Him and trust Him with every area of their lives.

No matter what you might be facing, it is time to tuck in your cloak and run faster.

When God is with you, it does not matter if others have horses, chariots, buggies, jalopies, SUVs or BMWs. You will outrun them all with the power of the Almighty. His Word tells us, "God's strong hand is on you; he'll promote you at the right time. Live carefree before God; he is most careful with you" (1 Peter 5:6–7 MSG).

You may have grown tired of waiting on God, but He will never give up on you. You may have let go of God, but He has never let go of you. You may even have stopped believing in God, but God has never stopped believing in you! He has equipped you for times such as these. Right now, you are about to receive a new outpouring of His Spirit that will sustain you for the next race to be run.

Yes, others will try and stop you. As we have seen, the devil will try to derail you and deride you and destroy you. But what heaven has launched, hell can never halt. Even if it appears fool-hardy to enter the race, to tuck and run, to expect anything other than second place, it is time to trust God and run. I love the way Peter coaches us to keep going no matter how many obstacles we may face:

> Keep a cool head. Stay alert. The Devil is poised to pounce, and would like nothing better than to catch you napping. Keep your guard up. You're not the only ones plunged into these hard times. It's the same with Christians all over the world. So keep a firm grip on the faith. The suffering won't last forever. It won't be long before this generous God who has great plans for us in Christ— eternal and glorious plans they are!—will have you put together and on your feet for good. He gets the last word; yes, he does.
>
> 1 Peter 5:8–11 MSG

When you run the good race to the full extent of the divine power bequeathed to you, then you can leave the results to God. You can know without a doubt that you are changing the future. Transparency precedes transformation. Transparent leaders pro-duce transparent followers. Never trip over your mantle, because others will inherit its power after you have crossed the finish line. They will do even greater things because of what you are doing right now, today.

Those who follow behind you will live different, better, holier lives because you have tucked your mantle and run the race of faith by relying on God's power and not your own.

Those who follow behind you will not inherit your sins—they will inherit your mantle!

Those who follow behind you will not inherit your mistakes— they will inherit your mantle!

Those who follow behind you will not inherit your debts—they will inherit your mantle!

God has been waiting for you to mature so that you can handle the power that comes with His mantle of promotion. You have pushed your plow. You have survived the drought and summoned the fire. You have watched for the rain and felt it falling on your face.

Now it is time to tuck and run—with the wind at your back and God's glorious future before you.

Push Your Plow, Meet Your Mantle

As you discover more of God's mantle for your life, you will also gain experience and wisdom about how to wear this mantle in a variety of situations. Like Elijah racing against Ahab, you will find the need to tuck your mantle away at times in order to run faster. You will need to surrender all that you have attained and been blessed to steward so that God can use you to run the race suddenly set before you. Your mantle is still there, but it may not be displayed the way you expect.

Use the questions below to help you reflect on the race you are currently running and what it means for you to tuck in order to run faster in the power of God's Spirit. More importantly, spend a few minutes in prayer and seek your Father's voice. Ask Him for the strength, stamina and support you need in order to do what He is calling you to do. Then tuck in whatever got you to this point so that you can have more mobility and travel faster.

1. When have you most recently been surprised by God's timing—either when He moved immediately or when you needed to wait? What has waiting on Him taught you about perseverance? About wearing your mantle of prophetic power and promotion?

2. When have you been required to persevere repeatedly, just like Elijah's servant looking to the sea, in order to glimpse what God wanted to give you? When has a "little cloud" in your life turned into a downpour of God's blessings?

3. What race in life are you currently running that requires supernatural power to keep going? In your relationships? With family? Close friends or coworkers? In your career or place of employment? At church or in your ministry? What does it mean for you to tuck your mantle so that you can run this race faster?

Dear Lord, forgive me for the excuses I have made for not trusting You or the times I have been impatient when You have actually been waiting on me to mature. I am so grateful for the ways You have revealed Your power and presence in my life—may I never overlook them or take You for granted. As You help me transition from my plow of perseverance to my mantle of promotion, give me wisdom about when to tuck and run despite the odds against me. I know that with You all things are possible! Thank You for the power to run the race of faith, knowing that You have prepared the way for me to finish and leave an eternal legacy for others. Amen.

7

Going from Gilgal

When God anoints you as His beloved child, the pain of your past can never compare to the prize of your future!

Some places symbolize the intersection of events, relationships and milestones in ways that transcend latitude and longitude. My wife and I, for example, enjoy returning to certain restaurants not because the cuisine is necessarily so delicious but because our memories of being there when we were dating will always season our meals there. Our children surprise us sometimes in their desire to return to places that apparently were special, even magical, for them in childhood, even when their mother and I fail to recall our visits there quite so fondly.

There is a sense of nostalgia in returning to such places, a blend of remembering the past and tracing your journey into the present with the particular locale as a launching pad or stopover along the way. Such return visits have been a human practice in ways both secular and sacred for hundreds if not thousands of years. Many such places feature unparalleled beauty or natural distinctions setting them apart, such as a mountain higher than those around it, like Mount Denali, or the stunning size of the giant redwoods of Northern California and the Pacific Northwest. The beauty and uniqueness make these places memorable unto themselves.

Other places draw return visitors not because of any natural features but events that happened there. These magnetically appealing locations commemorate historic events, such as Independence Hall in Philadelphia, the destination for many of my school field trips as a boy. In our country, you might think of Plymouth Rock, Mount Vernon, the White House and the Statue of Liberty. Other locations mark the spot where battles were fought or tragedies occurred, such as the shores of Normandy, where Allied Forces landed on D-Day during World War II, or Auschwitz, where millions of mostly Jewish prisoners were murdered.

Still other locales commanding return visits recall sacred events, heavenly miracles, divine prophecies and revelations. Not long after Jesus' resurrection and ascension into heaven, many of His followers began traveling to Jerusalem, Nazareth, Bethlehem, the Mount of Olives and the Sea of Galilee. They wanted to see the sites where He walked and talked, healed others and revealed Himself as the long-promised Messiah. Aware that God had literally lived as a man in these very locales, they eagerly traveled the same roads, visited the same synagogues, wandered through Gethsemane, and worshiped at Golgotha and the cave believed to have been His three-day tomb.

As Christianity spread, more and more visitors ventured to Israel, which soon became known as the Holy Land, to see the places where Jesus had spent His time on earth. By medieval times, believers extended their travels when possible to trace the routes of the apostle Paul and other disciples of Christ. Soon the birthplaces, ministry hubs and gravesites of other venerated saints and recognized giants of the faith began attracting visitors as well. Such travelers came to be known as pilgrims and their annual trips as pilgrimages.

One of the most famous in the world is the *Camino de Santiago*, known in English as the Way of Saint James or by many today as simply the Way. Located in northern Spain, where a number of ancient routes intersect, this network of trails, old Roman highways and footpaths ends in Galicia at a cathedral believed to contain the remains of Jesus' disciple James, the son of Zebedee and brother of the apostle John. According to legend, James' body was taken by boat from Jerusalem to Spain, a land he is believed to have evangelized. By the Middle Ages, the Way of Saint James was considered one of the most important pilgrimages, ranking right after Jerusalem and Rome.

Even before believers undertook any of these pilgrimages, however, the Bible indicates that some sites were designated as sacred by God Himself. Such is the case for Gilgal, a place identified in the Old Testament as memorable for several significant reasons—including a visit by Elijah and Elisha. Like Gilgal, certain places remind us where we used to be and where God is now leading us.

These are sacred places for leaving the past behind in order to embrace a glorious future.

Rolling Stones

Early in human history, God Himself sometimes designated certain locations as sacred to the people of Israel. Among them was Gilgal, which we are told Elijah and Elisha visited prior to their parting: "When the LORD was about to take Elijah up to heaven in a whirlwind, Elijah and Elisha were on their way from Gilgal" (2 Kings 2:1).

Prior to being whisked home to heaven by the Lord, Elijah visited several spiritually significant places, a kind of greatest-hits-of-Israel pilgrimage, we might say, major pit stops of great prophetic significance. As we will explore in the next chapters, three of these locations were Bethel, Jericho and Jordan—but the prophet's farewell tour began with Gilgal. And it was no coincidence whatsoever that Elijah began his trajectory there.

Gilgal was important to the people of Israel for three primary reasons. The first came after the death of Moses when Joshua was leading the children of Israel to the Promised Land. They crossed the Jordan River and established Gilgal as a monumental site to commemorate their crossing. The Lord had miraculously parted the waters of the Jordan—while the river was at flood stage, we are told (see Joshua 3:15)—so they could cross safely with the Ark of the Covenant, the sacred portable home of the Ten Commandments and a constant reminder of God's presence in their midst.

This parting of the Jordan called to mind the dramatic path God had earlier opened in the Red Sea when the Israelites were fleeing Egypt with Pharaoh's army in pursuit. Perhaps that was why God directed Joshua to establish Gilgal as an enduring reminder:

> When the whole nation had finished crossing the Jordan, the LORD said to Joshua, "Choose twelve men from among the people, one from each tribe, and tell them to take up twelve stones from the middle of the Jordan, from right where the priests are standing, and carry them over with you and put them down at the place where you stay tonight."
>
> So Joshua called together the twelve men he had appointed from the Israelites, one from each tribe, and said to them, "Go over before the ark of the LORD your God into the middle of the Jordan. Each of you is to take up a stone on his shoulder, according

to the number of the tribes of the Israelites, to serve as a sign among you. In the future, when your children ask you, 'What do these stones mean?' tell them that the flow of the Jordan was cut off before the ark of the covenant of the LORD. When it crossed the Jordan, the waters of the Jordan were cut off. These stones are to be a memorial to the people of Israel forever."

Joshua 4:1–7

Notice that even the twelve stones had symbolic value, each chosen by a representative on behalf of his tribe to signify the twelve tribes of God's chosen people. Notice, too, that these stones were selected from the middle of the dry riverbed, right where the priests remained standing holding the Ark of the Covenant until everyone had crossed safely and the commands of the Lord had been carried out. The display of curated river stones marked the occasion not only for the Hebrew participants but for all future generations as well, designated as "a memorial to the people of Israel *forever*" (Joshua 4:7, emphasis added).

This place was named Gilgal, however, because of a major event related to the monument of stones that occurred not long after the Israelites had crossed the Jordan and set up camp. You may recall that God had established circumcision as a powerful symbolic act of His covenant with His people, beginning with Abraham and the men of his household (see Genesis 17:10–14). The people of Israel had continued this divinely commanded ritual even after resettling in Egypt and their subsequent captivity there. So the Hebrew men Moses led through the Red Sea and into the desert had all been circumcised.

When the Israelites finally reached the Promised Land after their forty years' wandering in the desert, Moses had died and God had chosen Joshua to take command. By this time, "all the men who were of military age when they left Egypt had died, since they had not obeyed the LORD" (Joshua 5:6). The sons of these men, born during the four-decade trek through the desert, had not been circumcised. Consequently, before proceeding to take possession of the Promised Land, God instructed Joshua to resume the ritual: "Make flint knives and circumcise the Israelites again" (Joshua 5:2).

Afterward, God told Joshua, "Today I have rolled away the reproach of Egypt from you," which apparently is why the place came to be called Gilgal (Joshua 5:9). In Hebrew, the word for *roll* is similar to *Gilgal* both as a verb and a noun. Thus, the name refers to the circle of stones the Israelites had taken out of the riverbed, which were likely rolled into formation, as well as this explanatory message the Lord provided to Joshua about rolling away "the reproach of Egypt."

Crossroads for the Cross

This, then, was the second primary reason that Gilgal stood as an important place for Elijah to visit. It was the place where all the men who came into the Promised Land were circumcised in order to separate them from their past. Parenthetically speaking, the instructions coming from heaven implied a clear message to these younger generations: "Your parents didn't make it but you will." While their parents had disobeyed and rebelled against God, and, therefore, were not allowed to enter the Promised Land, these newly circumcised men were getting another chance, a fresh start. By requiring their circumcision, God indicated that they were once again being set apart from the reproach of the past. They were now accomplishing what their ancestors did not.

We all need a place like Gilgal on our journeys of faith. Gilgal is God's way of allowing us to come clean before Him and start anew. It is as if the calendar has been reset to start a new year, a fresh beginning, a reboot of the spiritual system we have been running in the hard drive of the soul. When we establish and claim Gilgal in our lives, we are not only creating an altar to praise and thank God for getting us to this point—we are also being reminded that God has completely separated us from who we used to be. We are no longer covered by the reproach, shame, guilt, fear and punishment of the past. Instead, we discover God's grace at our own personal Gilgal, a crossroads for the cross of Christ in our lives.

At Gilgal, you are completely separated from the old you, from the broken you, from the sinful you, from the defeated you. God is now telling you that there is nothing in your past that can stop your anointed future. This is the essence of the Good News of the Gospel of Jesus Christ: "Therefore, if anyone is in Christ, the new creation has come: The old has gone, the new is here!" (2 Corinthians 5:17).

You are no longer the liar you once were.

You are no longer the thief you once were.

You are no longer the cheater you once were.

You are no longer the gossip you once were.

You are no longer the fornicator you once were.

You are no longer the adulterer you once were.

You are no longer the coveter you once were.

You are no longer the murderer you once were.

You are no longer the self-righteous legalist you once were.

You are a new creature washed clean from all your iniquities of the past by the blood of the Lamb, Jesus Christ!

As you transition from pushing your plow of perseverance to wearing your mantle of promotion, God will lead you to Gilgal before you continue on your journey. There, He reminds you that you have been reborn, changed, set apart. There, at your own personal Gilgal, your heavenly Father whispers in your ear:

I am separating you.

I have rolled away the shame, the condemnation, the pain.

The pain of your past can never compare to the prize of your future.

The Holy Spirit reminds you that you have died to sin and been resurrected in grace. Along with the apostle Paul and other believers, you can proclaim, "I have been crucified with Christ and I no longer live, but Christ lives in me. The life I now live in the body, I live by faith in the Son of God, who loved me and gave himself for me" (Galatians 2:20).

When you reach Gilgal, God says you are not that person anymore. You are now His beloved son or daughter. You are not what you have done or left undone. You are not who others say you are or want you to be.

At Gilgal, God says He took *you* out of Egypt and He took *Egypt* out of you!

And there is more good news! Your children will never have to return to Egypt again. Your children and your children's children and your children's children's children will never live in what God took you out of! Those who follow after you will not be enslaved by the consequences of your sins. They will not have to carry the burden of their parents' sins because they have been set free.

Gilgal changes everything!

Just Grow Up

Gilgal also represents a third significant event in the lives of the Israelites. After they had crossed the Jordan River and rolled twelve stones together to form an eternal monument, after the Israelites had obeyed the Lord's instructions and been circumcised, they stayed at Gilgal long enough to heal and to celebrate Passover. Their celebration of Passover, and what occurred the next day, marked another turning point for the people of Israel:

> The day after the Passover, that very day, they ate some of the produce of the land: unleavened bread and roasted grain. The manna stopped the day after they ate this food from the land; there was no longer any manna for the Israelites, but that year they ate the produce of Canaan.
>
> Joshua 5:11–12

You will recall that during their forty-year sojourn in the wilderness the Israelites ate manna, similar to unleavened bread, which the Lord provided on a daily basis. Manna could not be collected and saved for later; each day's supply was intended to nourish people in the present only. Having finally reached Canaan, this long-awaited land flowing with milk and honey, the people went through another transition into maturation here at Gilgal. God no longer provided manna for them because they had arrived! They could eat the grains, fruits and meats in this bountiful land that the Lord had promised to them when leaving Egypt.

God's people had matured enough to trust Him because of His faithfulness. The Lord had taken care of them each step of the way, despite their rebellion, idolatry and bitter complaints. Now, the Almighty had made good on His promise and brought His people to the Promised Land of Canaan. In many ways, Gilgal was like a welcome station to commemorate such a monumental milestone. It was not their final destination but was a place to get their physical, emotional and spiritual bearings before exploring their new home.

Maybe you have stopped at one of those welcome centers as you crossed from one state to another and or one country to another. Residents want you to acknowledge that you are no longer in Kansas (or wherever) anymore but on their turf now. Most want you to feel welcome and to appreciate and enjoy the many resources, natural and otherwise, featured in their region.

Think of your Gilgal the same way—a kind of spiritual welcome center for the new life awaiting you. Because you are not where you used to be! And you no longer need the manna you used to rely on God to provide. You have matured and grown and developed spiritually so that you no longer need milk but are finally ready for meat. In his letter to the querulous church at Corinth, Paul pointed out that many of them were still "worldly—mere infants in Christ." As a result of delaying their own development, Paul explained, "I gave you milk, not solid food, for you were not yet ready for it" (1 Corinthians 3:1–2).

As you walk with the Lord and grow to trust Him in all areas of your life, you discover that you no longer need baby food. When you were a new Christian, so much was unfamiliar to you—prayer, God's Word, spiritual gifts, church, on and on. But as you obeyed Him and gained experience being led by His Holy Spirit, you developed spiritual muscle and gained maturity. As we have seen, moving from the plow to the mantle usually brings new responsibilities, including being a servant-leader to others. God's expectations are clear: "You have been believers so long now that you ought to be teaching others" rather than needing "someone to teach you again the basic things about God's word" (Hebrews 5:12 NLT).

If you want to experience all that God has for you, then it is time to grow up.

Gilgal marks the place where you are weaned from milk and instead mature enough to eat spiritual meat. You no longer need to have your hand held and your doubts dismissed—now you are called upon to hold others' hands and be their shoulder of faith to lean on. You no longer have to be taught the alphabet of grace and the basics of salvation and sanctification. Instead, you are ready to teach others and set the example for new believers.

Getting to Gilgal requires patience and trust in the Lord. It is a vista where you stop and look back over all you have experienced and how God has miraculously sustained you on each step of your journey. It is a monument to God's goodness, faithfulness and provision.

Leaving Gilgal requires courage and even more trust in the Lord. It is the first step toward the new and exciting adventures awaiting you around the next bend. It is the foundation for a future forged by mature faith.

Heading South

Now that we have explored the layers of symbolic and historic significance contained in Gilgal, let's return to Elijah and Elisha. You will recall that prior to being taken up to heaven, Elijah and his apprentice visited four major prophetic points of power: Gilgal, Bethel, Jericho and Jordan. The first, Gilgal, was for reasons that we now see more clearly.

Elijah was about to cross over from earth into heaven, just as the Israelites had crossed the Jordan into the Promised Land. Gilgal marked this point of transition, the place grounded in the grace and goodness of God. By returning to Gilgal first, Elijah respected its importance as foundational in his lifetime as God's prophet. It provided an opportunity to recall once again not only what God had done for the people of Israel historically but also for Elijah personally.

Because if you are thinking this was an easy journey for Elijah, then it is time to recall what happened between outracing Ahab's chariot in the rainstorm by tucking and running (see 1 Kings 18:45–46) and finding Elisha in the field plowing (see 1 Kings 19:19). The short answer is simple: Elijah completely fell apart! He was climbing a spiritual mountain one moment, and then the next, he was paralyzed by looking down and seeing how high he had climbed.

The trigger, as we touched on previously, was Queen Jezebel's death threat. Enraged that Elijah had not only won the sacrifice showdown at the altars but had also had the prophets of Baal killed, she was determined to make the prophet suffer. And she did not need to send someone to kill him but only to threaten him with being killed. Jezebel knew how to torment him far more effectively than if she had sent an assassin. With her threat consuming him,

> Elijah was afraid and ran for his life. When he came to Beersheba in Judah, he left his servant there, while he himself went a day's journey into the wilderness. He came to a broom bush, sat down under it and prayed that he might die. "I have had enough, LORD," he said. "Take my life; I am no better than my ancestors." Then he lay down under the bush and fell asleep.
>
> 1 Kings 19:3–5

Somehow, the queen's threat and his own fear became catalysts for calamity. After all that Elijah had seen God do, he suddenly appears to have lost faith. After enduring the drought, scorching the idol altar call, killing Baal's prophets and successfully outracing the king's chariot in the rain, Elijah suddenly came undone just because nasty Jezebel did what she did best. I cannot help but wonder if some kind of cumulative toll washed over him as he panicked and ran for his life, perhaps something similar to post-traumatic stress disorder experienced by so many today.

After racing Ahab to Jezreel, he covered the distance from there to Beersheba—roughly another hundred miles. Surely, the prophet was physically exhausted from so much running! Beersheba, located in the southern part of Judah, was the site where Abraham had made a covenant with Abimelech, a Philistine king, for water rights to the well there (see Genesis 21:25–31). It was about as far south as Elijah could go and still have access to shelter, food and water, which perhaps explains why he chose to leave his servant there. If the prophet was determined to keep running, then he was compassionate enough to consider his servant's survival.

From Beersheba, Elijah traveled another day's journey into the wilderness. Like the Israelites roaming in the desert after God's dramatic deliverance from Egypt, Elijah was apparently determined to go his own way. He finally stopped when he came to a broom bush, a kind of juniper-like shrub and one of the few sources of shade in the desert. There, Elijah told God how he felt, with raw honesty that is more than relevant today. "I'm done, Lord!" the prophet said. "I can't go on. I can't do this any longer. Let whatever happens, happens. I don't care anymore."

Can you relate? If we are honest, do we not all relate to such moments when we feel so exhausted, overwhelmed, depleted and discouraged that we are done? From my own experience, such times are often immediately following some of the most powerful, meaningful mountaintop experiences I have had with God. Times when I have witnessed His power in miraculous ways, when He has provided for our church in stunningly surprising ways, when He has given me influence with presidents and power brokers running our country.

Throughout the Bible we see numerous times when someone struggles and stumbles right after being used by God and having intimately experienced His presence and power. Noah obeyed God, built the Ark, survived the Flood—and then got drunk and naked in front of his sons (see Genesis 9:18–23). Abraham experienced God's blessing and favor but was scared enough to lie and say his wife, Sarah, was his sister (see Genesis 20). After all that Moses had experienced with the Lord, he still lost his temper and disobeyed God, costing him his entry into the Promised Land (see Numbers 20:2–12).

In the New Testament, the same pattern emerges in the lives of several saints. Peter promised his devotion to Jesus in Gethsemane but then a few hours later denied three times even knowing Him (see Luke 22:54–62). Thomas had followed Jesus for three years and witnessed numerous miracles but could not believe his Master had risen from the dead until he saw the nail holes in His hands (see John 20:24–29). Jesus Himself was tempted by the devil immediately after fasting and praying in the desert for forty days and nights, following His baptism by John the Baptist (Matthew 4:1–11).

Some scholars and experts believe Elijah exhibits the symptoms of what we would now label clinical depression—anxiety, despair, loneliness, meaninglessness, fear, sadness and a desire to die. While it may surprise us to consider such a possibility for such a giant of the faith, every human being, believers as well as nonbelievers, eventually experiences times of doubt, loss and stress. Such struggles do not necessarily invalidate our faith or indicate a lack of faith; they may simply be trials and temptations that can draw us closer to the Lord if we let them.

So before we are too critical of Elijah's desperate declaration, we should remember that most of us encounter such broom-bush moments in the wilderness before we reach Gilgal. And Elijah's example makes it clear that we can be honest with God—He already knows us better than we know ourselves. Sometimes, I suspect we tell Him as a way of expressing what we have been running from.

"What Are You Doing Here?"

God's response to Elijah's suicidal soliloquy always amazes me, although I should not be surprised by such love, compassion and personal concern from our heavenly Father. First, the Lord sent an angel to awaken Elijah so that he could nourish his body with bread, baked over hot coals beside him, and water from a jar. The prophet did as instructed and fell asleep again.

Then the angel returned and made sure Elijah ate and drank once again because the prophet had a divine appointment with God at Mount Horeb (see 1 Kings 19:6–8). We are not certain how far this distance was, but we do know it took Elijah forty days and nights to get there. Upon arrival he went in a cave to spend the night. Before we go spelunking with Elijah, though, note what had to happen even before he had a conversation with God.

Rather than rebuke Elijah and tell him to quit complaining, God sent a messenger to provide food and water. While it is obvious to us that the prophet was exhausted and probably malnourished, which in turn affected his dire emotional state, Elijah had reached a point where he could no longer help himself. So God began with the basics. Before instructing Elijah to meet Him at Horeb, the Lord knew that His prophet needed to recover physically.

Sometimes we become distraught and overwhelmed by our feelings simply because we fail to take proper care of our bodies, which in turn leaves us feeling even worse, both physically and emotionally. In our 21st-century world of being online 24/7, people are busier than ever—if not working, then surfing online to shop, read, be entertained or connect on social media.

We push our bodies well past our limits by working harder and sleeping less, and then wonder why we cannot rest when we finally collapse. We rarely eat nutritiously or exercise, and our bodies pay the price. And we also suffer mentally, emotionally and spiritually, often running to hide in our own caves of desperation, discouragement and depression.

Based on Elijah's experience, however, God still meets us in those dark places of pain. Once the prophet reached Horeb, God asked him, "What are you doing here?" (1 Kings 19:9)—a funny question since Elijah had followed the Lord's instruction to meet Him there. Of course, the question transcends geography because God in His divine wisdom was helping His prophet come to terms with His malaise.

Elijah replied by sharing the burden weighing on his heart: "I have been very zealous for the Lord God Almighty. The Israelites have rejected your covenant, torn down your altars, and put your prophets to death with the sword. I am the only one left, and now they are trying to kill me too" (1 Kings 19:10). Can you hear his frustration? There is a sense of futility, almost as if saying, "Look, God, I've devoted my life to serving You—but what difference has it made? The Israelites are still rebelling and turning away from You. They've killed all Your prophets except me—and now they're going to kill me, too!"

Rather than come down on Elijah for feeling this way, God directed His prophet to go stand at the mouth of the cave there on Mount Horeb because God was about to pass by. Outside, the natural forces of the earth must have seemed to go berserk! A tremendous wind tore the mountains apart and shattered rocks, followed by an earthquake and fire. Poor Elijah heard the cacophony of nature's calamity outside. Then when he heard a gentle whisper, "he pulled his cloak over his face and went out and stood at the mouth of the cave" (1 Kings 19:13).

In the presence of God, sometimes our only response can be to use our mantle as a protective mask. During the COVID-19 pandemic, people learned to wear masks in order to protect themselves and others from contracting the virus. When God gives us a mantle of promotion, sometimes we realize that it provides protection from the limitless power accessible to us through God's Spirit within us.

After the dramatic display of God's presence, once again the Lord asked, "What are you doing here, Elijah?" (1 Kings 19:13). When the prophet repeated his first answer, God gave Elijah his next mission:

> The LORD said to him, "Go back the way you came, and go to the Desert of Damascus. When you get there, anoint Hazael king over Aram. Also, anoint Jehu son of Nimshi king over Israel, and anoint Elisha son of Shaphat from Abel Meholah to succeed you as prophet. Jehu will put to death any who escape the sword of Hazael, and Elisha will put to death any who escape the sword of Jehu. Yet I reserve seven thousand in Israel—all whose knees have not bowed down to Baal and whose mouths have not kissed him."
>
> 1 Kings 19:15–18

God supplied a subtle rebuttal to Elijah's declaration, making it clear that Elijah was not the only faithful prophet left alive—in fact, there were seven thousand still going strong! On top of that, Elijah was not going to be killed because God had a job for him, basically to go back the way he came and find his successor, Elisha.

Rather than telling Elijah not to feel that way, the Lord gave him something significant to do.

This remedy continues to be one of the best, most effective cures whenever we are struggling. Our enemy likes to use those opportunities to play on our emotions in hopes we will feel sorry for ourselves and give in to temptation. But when we take our focus off of ourselves and our feelings, we discover the joy that comes from using our God-given gifts to serve others. We discover the maturity that comes with wearing the mantle.

Which brings us full circle back to Gilgal. After enduring such an excruciating season of depression, Elijah went on to mentor Elisha and prepare him for the time when he would be on his own. So as they anticipated God taking Elijah to heaven, they made one last holy pilgrimage together. It had been a curving, crazy road to get there, but when following God, they knew it was worthwhile.

We must remember the same truth, my friend. As we transition into wearing the mantle of promotion, we often find that a quick glimpse of Gilgal fortifies us with faith for where the Lord will lead us next. Such visits remind us that we are no longer residents of our past but citizens of a glorious, heavenly future.

Push Your Plow, Meet Your Mantle

We all go through seasons of discouragement in which we question our purpose and feel limited by harsh circumstances. Even then, however, we can trust that God is leading through these times for the purpose of strengthening our faith and preparing us for our next mission, just as He did with Elijah. While we may run away or hide in our caves temporarily, God will meet us there and remind us that we are no longer in Egypt, no longer wandering in the wilderness in search of home.

Use the questions below to help you get your bearings as you press on toward your mantle of promotion. Then spend a few minutes in prayer, asking God to meet you wherever you are on your journey. Just as He revealed himself to Elijah, God delights in showing you who He really is and how much He cares for you.

1. When you look back on your journey of faith, what strikes you as a place like Gilgal, one that signaled your transition from your old self to becoming a new creature in Christ? Have you ever revisited this place? Would you like to? Why or why not?

2. When have you struggled with discouragement and doubt that seemed to pull you into depression? How did you handle those feelings during that experience? How did God meet you in the midst of it all?

3. What mission is God revealing to you lately? Where is He calling you to serve next? How does reflecting on your own Gilgal reinforce this direction?

Dear God, I'm so grateful for how You have sustained me, nourished me and empowered me, especially in times when I feared I could not keep going. Never allow me to be so consumed by my emotions that I lose sight of You and Your love for me. Help me to take my eyes off my own struggles and focus on the example of Jesus as I seek to meet the needs of others. I am excited to see where You are leading me next, Lord, and what my journey of faith holds as You wrap me in Your mantle of prophetic promotion. May all I do be through You, for You and with You! To God be the glory! Amen.

8

Eyes on the Prize

When you wear the mantle of promotion, you discover your hard place will become your high place—failure is not an option!

Recently I went online to order some new running shoes only to discover that my favorites had been retired. The company making them had replaced them with an "improved" new version. But as I read the description of this fourth-generation model, I realized it no longer had the key features that made its predecessor my favorite.

Once again, because this had happened before in recent years, I would need to visit a sporting goods store and try on a variety of running shoes in order to find *the one* destined to make me lighter, faster and stronger. Unless new running shoes now had built-in rocket boosters—such an improvement being unlikely!— I at least wanted something that would provide adequate support, flexibility and comfort. That should not be so hard to find, should it?

A couple of years had passed since I had actually been in a store to try on running shoes. Like many of us, I had been spoiled by the convenience of ordering online, especially since I knew exactly what I wanted. Now, strolling down the aisle to the runners' merchandise, I faced an entire wall of possibilities. Some could be ruled out quickly, but others commanded consideration. And I soon realized that the science of running had been forced into an arranged marriage with marketers in order to produce more features, options and styles than ever before. In fact, I could literally design my own running shoe using the in-store digital design system.

Did I want extreme, moderate or light cushion in the heel? Did I want smooth soles, for less friction and more speed, or treaded soles for traction when trail running outdoors? How much shock absorption should the sole support provide? When my feet hit the ground, was my gait suffering from underpronation or overpronation? Or did I have neutral pronation? Were my ankles weak or my arches fallen? In order to buy the right running shoe, I had to know.

Then there was the question of style. As a kid who, until high school, had no idea that running shoes came in any color but white, I now had the full spectrum from which to choose. Nike, Saucony and ASICS in white were outnumbered by blue, red, gray and orange Adidas, Brooks and New Balance. And once the shoe color was selected, then I could decide about contrasting trim and the color of the soles, as well as the laces, of course.

Not surprisingly, I was completely overwhelmed! Based on the look of the young, lean Olympic sprinter slumming as a sales rep, I was clearly not a serious runner. Even worse, I sensed he thought I was not merely old school but just old. After trying on at least six different pairs, I left the store without purchasing any new running shoes.

Too many options can often be more frustrating than lack of options.

I got sidetracked from my goal—to exercise by doing something I enjoy, running—and lost my focus.

I momentarily took my eyes off the prize!

Have It Your Way

Running shoes are not the only branded items offering us more options. Most people in highly developed First World nations likely have more consumer options than any human beings throughout history. From the kind of jeans we wear to the flavors of mustard, our 21st-century world provides an array of possibilities for purchase. Whether we simply want jeans that finally fit our bodies just right or wish to serve gourmet Dijon to express our superb culinary taste, we can have it our way, as the Burger King jingle used to promise us when I was a kid.

More possibilities, however, do not necessarily make our lives easier. In fact, some experts believe that our culture likely reached a retail-marketing saturation point some years ago. In 2000, a pair of psychologists published the results of a study they conducted involving consumer choices. They set up a display at an upscale food store featuring 24 different varieties of gourmet jam. Customers could sample as many as they liked and in return receive a coupon for one dollar off any jam purchase.

After recording the number of participants and the number of coupons both issued and redeemed, the researchers returned a few days later and set up their taste-sampling display once again, but this time with only six kinds of jam. Although more consumers stopped at the display with more varieties, few used their coupons to make a purchase. Customers sampling the half-dozen varieties of jam, however, were ten times more likely to buy a jar.[1]

Other social and psychological studies have recorded similar findings. Having more choices often complicates our decisions to the point that we defer making one. With so many options, we fear making the "wrong" choice and wasting money on uncertain varieties. Writing in the *Harvard Business Review*, one expert points out, "As the variety of snacks, soft drinks, and beers offered at convenience stores increases, for instance, sales volume and customer satisfaction decrease."[2]

What does all this have to do with moving from your plow to your mantle?

Everything!

You have too many options demanding your attention, pulling you from your path to promotion. Because you will never leave your plow behind and be ready to accept the mantle of promotion if you do not keep your eyes on the prize. Even the most passionate, dedicated followers of Jesus can be pulled in too many directions as distractions divert their attention and dilute their energy: Having too many options vying for our attention is not simply a problem for sales and marketing.

We live in an age when we are told that we can have everything, try everything and be whoever we want, whenever we want. But this is simply not true! God created us in His own holy image and knows us better than we know ourselves. Only a relationship with Him can ever satisfy our deepest core longings for love, intimacy and purpose.

1. Sheena S. Iyengar and Mark R. Lepper, "When Choice is Demotivating: Can One Desire Too Much of a Good Thing?," *Journal of Personality and Social Psychology*, no. 6 (2000): 995–1006.

2. Barry Schwartz, "More Isn't Always Better," *Harvard Business Review*, June 2006, https://hbr.org/2006/06/more-isnt-always-better.

The enemy of our souls thrives on today's glossy package of lies because it keeps us from focusing on what is true, what is real, what is eternal. If we can be conned into thinking that we can control our lives, then we have no need to rely on God's power and trust His guidance on a daily basis. We can have a polite faith of distance and detachment. But it pales in comparison to a passionate relationship with the Spirit of the living God dwelling in us.

In order to move forward in our God-given purpose and grow in our faith, we must focus exclusively on Jesus. We must immerse ourselves in God's Word and become attuned to the voice of the Holy Spirit. All priorities must begin and end with our relationship with the Lord. Otherwise, we remain susceptible to distractions, even though often for good reasons and urgent causes. The apostle Paul pursued this kind of singularity of focus and inspires us to do the same:

> I want to know Christ—yes, to know the power of his resurrection and participation in his sufferings, becoming like him in his death, and so, somehow, attaining to the resurrection from the dead.
>
> Not that I have already obtained all this, or have already arrived at my goal, but I press on to take hold of that for which Christ Jesus took hold of me. Brothers and sisters, I do not consider myself yet to have taken hold of it. But one thing I do: Forgetting what is behind and straining toward what is ahead, I press on toward the goal to win the prize for which God has called me heavenward in Christ Jesus.
>
> Philippians 3:10–14

The secret to keeping our eyes on the prize is revealed by that last verse. Notice that Paul reduces his focus to "one thing," moving forward by "forgetting what is behind and straining toward what is ahead." This is the same journey Elijah took with Elisha prior to being taken up to heaven by the Lord. As we saw in the last chapter, they visited Gilgal and then "they went down to Bethel" (2 Kings 2:2).

Why go to Bethel next?

Because if Gilgal is about recognizing the hard places in your life, then Bethel is about holding on to your dream.

Climbing Jacob's Ladder

As you have likely learned by now, every detail recorded in God's Word carries significance, both as a literal record of history and as a timeless metaphor applied to human lives into our present moment. Such is the case with the prophets' stops on Elijah's farewell tour. Tracing the footsteps of Elijah and Elisha, we explored the origin and symbolism of Gilgal, so now we walk with them to Bethel, likely a distance of about seven miles depending on their route.

Bethel, which means "house of God," holds a special place in the history of Israel because of the nation's namesake patriarch. First known as *Jacob* before God changed his name, this man often seemed to take one step forward and two steps backward in his spiritual journey. But God had a special, life-changing purpose for Jacob and always met him in the midst of his messes. Along the way, Jacob received glimmers of hope from heaven that motivated him even when obstacles seemed to block his life's path. Such is the case during a very special night while traveling:

Jacob left Beersheba and set out for Harran. When he reached a certain place, he stopped for the night because the sun had set. Taking one of the stones there, he put it under his head and lay down to sleep. He had a dream in which he saw a stairway resting on the earth, with its top reaching to heaven, and the angels of God were ascending and descending on it. There above it stood the LORD, and he said: "I am the LORD, the God of your father Abraham and the God of Isaac. I will give you and your descendants the land on which you are lying. Your descendants will be like the dust of the earth, and you will spread out to the west and to the east, to the north and to the south. All peoples on earth will be blessed through you and your offspring. I am with you and will watch over you wherever you go, and I will bring you back to this land. I will not leave you until I have done what I have promised you."

When Jacob awoke from his sleep, he thought, "Surely the LORD is in this place, and I was not aware of it." He was afraid and said, "How awesome is this place! This is none other than the house of God; this is the gate of heaven."

Early the next morning Jacob took the stone he had placed under his head and set it up as a pillar and poured oil on top of it. He called that place Bethel, though the city used to be called Luz.

Genesis 28:10–19

Keep in mind that Jacob had left home after maneuvering his twin brother, Esau, out of his birthright and then deceiving their father, Isaac, into blessing him with what was rightfully not Jacob's to receive (see Genesis 27). Esau, furious over being cheated out of his rightful blessing, vowed to kill his brother, which prompted their mother, Rebekah, to send Jacob on the road to stay with her brother, Laban, in Harran until Esau cooled down (see Genesis 27:42–43).

So here was Jacob, running away from one set of family problems and about to run into another (marrying sisters Leah and Rachel), when God gave him a dream of his divine destiny. And what a destiny! No matter how badly Jacob had blown it back in Beersheba or how terribly relationships were about to fray in Harran, he had a God-given dream to realize. Jacob knew he could let go of his past because God had revealed his future.

Climbing the ladder to his dreams would make stretching for each rung worth it.

Traveling from Gilgal to Bethel, the site of Jacob's dream, Elijah and Elisha symbolically bridged the past and the future. Just as Jacob watched the movie trailer for the epic legacy he would leave, Elijah ventured to Bethel knowing he was about to go to his ultimate destination, his heavenly home with God. His journey to Bethel, along with Jacob's dream there, reminds us that we, too, reside between the struggles of the past and the dream of the future.

Just like Jacob, just like Elijah, you are about to see what you have never seen before.

You begin at the altar.

You begin at the place of separation from your past.

And after you are separated from your past, then you are allowed to dream.

When you are living in your past, you do not have a dream—you have an illusion. You are running in place, stuck on a treadmill of your own making. This is not plowing with perseverance but rather digging a rut that only grows deeper the more you rely on your own power rather than God's. This is not preparing for your mantle of promotion but rather procrastinating because of past commotion.

But after you visit Gilgal . . .

After you have been to the cross of Christ . . .

After you have been washed by the blood of the Lamb . . .

Then your hard place becomes your high place.

When you leave Gilgal behind, when you allow God to give you His dream for your life, then the pain of your past becomes the hope for a better future.

You cross from the wilderness into the Promised Land.

Your nightmare is replaced by a dream.

You and your family glimpse heaven coming down.

Through the power of the Holy Spirit, this is the decade your dream becomes reality.

This is the year you will take a giant stride toward realizing the dream that God has planted inside you.

This is the month you will trust Him to show you more of His purpose for your life.

This is the day you will surrender all you have been holding back, all you have been grasping in your own power, and take His hand.

This is the moment, right here and right now even as you read the words on this page, that you decide whether you will delay the glorious adventure God has for you or take the next step. I do not know the reason you picked up this book. But I do know that it was not by accident!

I dare say it is time for you to move forward in seeing your dream come alive.

Gilgal is gone and now you are bound for Bethel!

Dream Weaving

When the ladder of your dreams appears before you, it changes your life, because you are no longer where you used to be—you are on your way up. When God gives you His dream for your life, then nothing can stop you from ascending toward higher places. Your climb probably will not be easy, but it will lead to things you have never seen before or even imagined.

Others may treat you differently because dreamers are dangerous. Jacob discovered this as he dealt with his brother, his uncle, his wives and his children. Joseph, who was Jacob's favorite son, learned the hard way that your dreams can make others jealous. But when you steward faithfully all that God gives you, your dreams can also save you. Joseph, sold into slavery by his brothers, was summoned from prison, where he landed after being falsely accused by Potiphar's wife, in order to interpret Pharaoh's dreams. Because of Joseph's gifts as a dreamer, he not only explained what Pharaoh's dreams meant but became second-in-command in all of Egypt.

Another Joseph was a dreamer, a carpenter from Nazareth engaged to a young virgin named Mary. When she was chosen to be the mother of Jesus, Joseph planned to do the honorable thing and discreetly call off their engagement. But he received a message from God in a dream that instructed him to honor his pledge to Mary and to proceed with their marriage, which he did. Later, after Mary had given birth to Christ in Bethlehem, Joseph was warned by a dream to flee to Egypt in order to escape from King Herod.

God has always used dreams and dreamers to accomplish His purposes—and He still does! His Word tells us, "In the last days, God says, I will pour out my Spirit on all people. Your sons and daughters will prophesy, your young men will see visions, your old men will dream dreams" (Acts 2:17). This promise reminds us that we not only dream for ourselves, but we also dream for our children, for our children's children, for our community, for our nation.

Divine dreamers help other people's dreams come true. They know that in order to keep their eyes on the prize, they must hold on to the key people God has placed in their lives. These individuals are often dream weavers, supporting and encouraging, learning and growing as they prepare to fulfill their own divine dreams.

Dreamers and dream weavers help each other keep their eyes on the prize. While Elijah kept telling Elisha to "stay here" before setting off for his next location, Elisha kept insisting, "I will not leave you" (2 Kings 2:2, 4, 6). Elijah perhaps wanted to prepare his apprentice for the time when they would no longer be together, grooming Elisha to take the mantle as God's prophet. Elisha, however, refused to abandon his mentor because of his commitment to Elijah and to the Lord.

When Elijah told Elisha to stay, he was also testing him. Although God had led Elijah to this young man in the fields, the prophet perhaps wanted one last confirmation of Elisha's dedication to the job. If Elisha remained committed to Elijah, then the younger prophet would remain committed to God after Elijah departed for heaven. As we transition from our plow to our mantle, I suspect we all get tested the same way.

How many times have you passed that test?

How many times have you failed that test?

Will you stay in that one season?

Will you stay in that one experience?

Will you be satisfied with that singular moment?

Will you become complacent?

Will you get comfortable?

Will you stay here in this moment, in this season, in this chapter—no matter what happens?

Will you be satisfied with just this?

Elisha could have chosen to obey his teacher and remain behind. But Elisha had matured enough to say, "No! Wherever you go, I will go."

If this experience had been painful and disruptive, perhaps he might have heeded Elijah's instruction to stay back. When others protect us or sacrifice for us, it is easy to convince ourselves we can stay put. But as believers, as children of the cross, as those designated to live life and life abundantly, we get tested all the time not between bad and good, but between good and great.

Not between failure and success.

But between surviving and thriving.

Some people get stuck in good when God has something great.

Some people get stuck surviving when God wants them thriving.

Some people get stuck in status quo when God wants to shake things up.

Do not get stuck!

Do not get stuck in a moment, in an experience, in one chapter, in one season. No matter how good it seems, to stay there when God calls you forward is a step backward. The Lord has more for you. Trust Him that the dream weavers in your life are there to accompany you on your spiritual journey. This is not the time to be satisfied with being sidelined. Never settle for less than God's best for your life.

The only way to resist settling is to keep your eyes on the prize.

You must stay focused and want more—more of God in every area of your life:

More of His presence.

More of His glory.

More of His power.

More of His love.

More of His truth.

More of His character.

More of His wisdom.

More of His favor.

More of His blessings.

More of the Father.

More of the Son.

More of His Holy Spirit!

When you keep your focus on the Lord and accept his mantle of promotion, then you not only receive more but give more. More is expected from you. Jesus said, "From everyone who has been given much, much will be demanded; and from the one who has been entrusted with much, much more will be asked" (Luke 12:48).

And when you have your eyes on the eternal prize, then you should warn everyone around you. You should be prepared to swim in an overflowing tide of blessings. Because when you wear the mantle of promotion and commit to going the distance, you will receive more than you can ever imagine.

When you reach a certain point and move from Gilgal to Bethel, then enough is no longer adequate in the eyes of the Lord. He is a God able to do exceedingly, abundantly, above and beyond anything and everything we could ever imagine or expect to receive. "Now to him who is able to do immeasurably more than all we ask or imagine, according to his power that is at work within us, to him be glory in the church and in Christ Jesus throughout all generations, for ever and ever!" (Ephesians 3:20–21).

When you reach a Bethel milestone, then God will fulfill your dreams and give you more dreams. He will give you more of who He is and empower you as a conduit of His more for others.

More of Him and less of you means more purpose, power and peace in your life:

More people saved.

More people delivered.

More people healed.

More people set free.

More people baptized with the Holy Spirit.

More casting out devils, more shifting of the atmosphere, more turning the world upside down for the glory of Jesus!

Failure Is Not an Option

Every single person on the planet today is on a spiritual journey. Each one of us is either failing or sailing, walking by faith or stuck in place, surviving or thriving. If you feel unable to move beyond your plow, to accept the mantle of promotion God has for you, then perhaps it is time to reconsider your focus. Are you looking down when you should be looking up?

Throughout the Bible we see lessons revealing why people fail. We learn from Adam and Eve in the Garden that we fail when we listen to the opinions of others and disobey the commands of God. We learn from Cain that envy is a portal for failure.

We learn from Lot's wife that we fail whenever we look back.

We learn from Samson that we fail if we find comfort in the facade of beauty called deception.

We learn from King Saul that we fail when we grieve and quench the Holy Spirit.

We learn from Judas that we fail when we settle for living in the presence of Jesus but never permit the presence of Jesus to live in us.

Even if we have not read and learned these lessons from Scripture, once we invite Jesus into our lives and His Spirit into our hearts, then failure is not an option.

For born-again believers, failure is not an option.

For the redeemed of the Lord, failure is not an option.

For those who have been washed by the blood of the Lamb Jesus Christ, failure is not an option.

For people filled with the Holy Spirit, failure is not an option. This is not my audacious claim—this is God's holy promise!

According to God, the One who knew you before you were born, you are not a failure.

Not only are you not a failure, but you will never live in failure.

Not only are you not a failure and not only will you never live in failure, but your children and your children's children and your children's children's children will never be failures or live in failure.

When you are in God's hands, how can you live in failure? His Word promises us this: "From eternity to eternity I am God. No one can snatch anyone out of my hand. No one can undo what I have done" (Isaiah 43:13 NLT). Jesus assures His children with these words: "I give them eternal life, and they shall never perish; no one will snatch them out of my hand" (John 10:28).

Repeat after me: "As for me and my house, failure is not an option. I reject failure; I rebuke failure; I refute failure; I refuse failure. We are not failures, and we will never live in failure."

But what about when we stumble? What about the times we fall?

Even when we fall, we fall within the confines of the shadow of the Almighty.

We fall in grace and in the hand of God.

Falling is not failure when you are in the hands of God.

Soul Survivors

Elijah knew firsthand that his falling was not his failure, a truth he then passed on to Elisha. Elijah had seen God do astounding, amazing, awe-inspiring miracles, and yet the prophet still got scared, still ran away, still hid in a cave. Even there, in the darkness of Elijah's fear, exhaustion, anxiety and despair, God met him. God still provided for him and restored not only Elijah's body but his spirit.

Elijah knew what it meant to be a soul survivor the way we are all soul survivors.

We have all been through things.

We all share some common elements that bind all survivors.

Many of us if not all have scars, some visible and some not.

But you only have to recall Jacob's limp or the scars on the hands of Jesus to realize that your scars do not disqualify you.

Your scars remind you that you are an overcomer.

Your scars remind you that if God did it before, He can do it again.

Survivors are more compassionate when they see others going through storms.

Survivors are less judgmental and more understanding.

Survivors praise a little differently.

Survivors pray a little differently.

Survivors worship a little differently.

Survivors preach a little differently.

Survivors prophesy a little differently.

Survivors have a testimony that serves as proof that the devil is a liar.

Hell said that you would not survive that spiritual drought, but you did.

Hell said that you would not survive that holy fire, but you did.

Hell said that you would not survive that storm, but you did.

How did you survive? Because the Lord was with you! He said, "When you go through deep waters, I will be with you. When you go through rivers of difficulty, you will not drown. When you walk through the fire of oppression, you will not be burned up; the flames will not consume you" (Isaiah 43:2 NLT).

When you have survived life's trials and tribulations, when you have suffered unexpected losses, when you have been through addiction and broken relationships, when you have come through all the abuse, betrayal and neglect others have thrown at you, then you know that failure is not an option. Your eyes are on the prize, and God's power makes you unstoppable. You may be forced to slow down, take a detour, stop to catch your breath or seek a new direction. But you cannot be stopped, any more than Elisha could be stopped from accompanying Elijah in his final days.

Soul survivors are Bethel believers! They know that even their worst moments can be redeemed by God for His purposes and for His glory. They are living, breathing examples of God's love in action, knowing the ultimate truth: "We are convinced that every detail of our lives is continually woven together to fit into God's perfect plan of bringing good into our lives, for we are his lovers who have been called to fulfill his designed purpose" (Romans 8:28 TPT).

Survivors know that as they mature in their faith, they become thrivers!

Thrive on the Prize

Unfortunately, many people get lost on the road between Gilgal and Bethel. Instead of making the transition from surviving to thriving, from the wilderness to the Promised Land, too many people cling to the past. When you are stuck in place, you condition yourself to just getting by. You stop dreaming and hoping and trusting God each day. And as your faith evaporates, you die in the desert. Too many people refuse to step out in faith even as they are dying of thirst for the living water that Jesus gives so generously.

Too many die in the desert of excuses.

Too many die in the desert of "if only."

Too many die in the desert of narcissism.

Too many die in the desert of perpetual victimization.

Too many die in the desert of dependency.

Too many die in the desert of procrastination.

Too many die in the desert of sin.

Too many die in the desert of fleshly living.

Too many die in the desert of lies.

My friend, it is time to reclaim the dreams of Bethel in your life.

It is time to refuse to die in the desert of disappointment, disillusionment and distraction.

It is time to thrive in the abundant land of milk and honey, of hope and love and faith.

This contrast is best summed up by Jesus Himself: "A thief has only one thing in mind—he wants to steal, slaughter, and destroy. But I have come to *give you everything in abundance, more than you expect*—life in its fullness until you overflow!" (John 10:10 TPT).

Surviving is a temporary season.

Thriving is a permanent lifestyle.

To survive you must learn to climb out of hell.

To thrive you must learn to climb the ladder of your heavenly dreams.

Surviving is about overcoming.

Thriving is about overflowing.

To survive you must fight off your enemies.

To thrive you must fight off yourself—your doubts, fears and complacency!

Surviving requires grace.

Thriving demands holiness.

To survive you must discover that there is power in the blood of Jesus.

To thrive you must live in the certainty of power in the name of Christ.

Surviving requires confessing and believing.

Thriving requires worshiping in Spirit and in truth.

To survive you must ask God to forgive your sins.

To thrive you must learn to forgive those who sinned against you.

Surviving is about getting the blessing.

Thriving is about *becoming* the blessing.

To survive you must look in the mirror.

To thrive you must look out the window.

Surviving requires a clean heart.

Thriving demands a renewed mind.

To survive is walking with Jacob's limp.

To thrive is climbing up Jacob's ladder.

Surviving is manna and water in the desert.
Thriving is milk and honey in the Promised Land.

To survive, the glory must fill the Temple.
To thrive, the latter glory must always be greater than the
former glory.

Surviving is about building altars.
Thriving is about tearing false altars down.

Surviving is about the cross.
Thriving is about the resurrection.

Surviving is about the process.
Thriving is about the outcome.

Surviving is God changing you.
Thriving is you in Christ changing the world!

Surviving looks down to the ground.
Thriving keeps your eyes on the prize!

Push Your Plow, Meet Your Mantle

Use these questions and the starter prayer below as an opportunity to pause, eliminate distractions, and still your heart before your heavenly Father. Turn off your phone, close your screen, shut your laptop and try to give Him your full, undivided attention. As you begin to reflect and share your heart, listen carefully for the whisper of the Holy Spirit. Think about what you need to eliminate in order to focus more on your relationship with God and keep your eyes on the prize.

1. What are the biggest distractions in your life right now? What pulls your attention away from focusing on your relationship with the Lord? What needs to change in order to adjust your priorities?

2. What dreams have you put on hold because you have gotten stuck instead of trusting God more and moving into a place of thriving? What dream is He leading you to pursue and realize right now?

3. What does it mean for you to keep your eyes on the prize as you walk by faith and not by sight during the current season of your life? What is required for you to be able to relinquish the past and live the abundant life He has for you?

Dear Lord, thank You for the many gifts of life abundant that You have already poured into my life. Forgive me when I take Your blessings for granted or allow my needs to come before the needs of others. May I be a good steward of all You entrust to me now and in the future. I am so grateful for the other dreamers and dream weavers You have placed in my life. Give us all the strength to continue on our journeys like Elijah and Elisha, refusing to leave each other behind. I refuse to die in the desert of past mistakes and stumbles. I know that I may fall but never fail because my life is in Your hands. May all I do be for Your glory and honor, my King! Amen.

9

The Jericho Promise and the Jordan Discovery

When you cannot see a way forward, God makes a way so that every wall becomes your bridge!

When a promise is fulfilled, you discover the power to persevere.

When you are living in the promise, it can be challenging, frustrating or overwhelming to wait for its fulfillment. But as you experience the prophetic power that comes with your mantle of promotion, your discovery leads to the next step and then the next.

Think of it this way. When Eva and I entered into holy matrimony as husband and wife, we made vows to one another. During our wedding ceremony, we committed to each other exclusively and promised to love, cherish, honor and serve one another. There at the altar on our wedding day, our vows expressed our love and the desire of our hearts before God and others.

But our lifetime promise to one another had not been fulfilled or tested yet because our marriage journey had just started. Now that we have been married more than twenty years, we have discovered what our commitment to one another actually means. By the grace of God and the patience of my beautiful bride, we have not experienced most of the trials, trauma and turmoil that test many in their marriages. It certainly has not been easy—even the best marriages require work, sacrifice and complete dedication—but next to my relationship with the Lord, loving Eva and being loved by her has had the greatest impact on my life.

When a promise of God is fulfilled, you discover new power, new peaks and new pathways. As God reveals His presence, overcomes all obstacles and creates a way where you cannot see one, you begin to trust Him more and more. Your love grows and you become more patient, more willing to wait, more obedient to His ways even when they do not conform to human logic, timing or rationale.

Miracles are never predictable, but they can be expected when you live in the power of the Lord. When your resources are depleted, God provides all you need. When life throws you a curve ball, God empowers you to hit it out of the park. When you see no way forward, God opens a path. When you hit a wall, God makes a bridge.

Friend or Foe

After leaving Gilgal and Bethel, Elijah announced that Jericho was his next stop. Once again, he told Elisha to stay behind while he went alone, and once again Elisha insisted, "As surely as the LORD lives and you yourself live, I will never leave you" (2 Kings 2:4 NLT). Notice the doubly conditional way Elisha worded his declaration—as surely as God lives and as surely as Elijah lived. God has always and will always live, so Elisha was indicating that his commitment to his mentor was timeless. Paradoxically, the only limit on it in that moment depended on their remaining moments together before God brought Elijah to heaven that day.

And Elisha knew that Elijah's time on earth was drawing to a close because the visits of these two renowned prophets of the Lord did not go unnoticed. In both Bethel and Jericho, the group of prophets in each area gathered and asked Elisha, "Do you know that the Lord is going to take your master from you today?" And each time, Elisha answered, "Yes, I know, so be quiet" (see 2 Kings 2:3, 5). The repetitive scene strikes me as comical, with the local prophets eager to tell the visiting prophet what he already knew was about to happen.

With God nothing is coincidental, and certainly not their visit to Jericho. Just as Gilgal and Bethel held significant spiritual history, Jericho did as well. After Joshua shepherded the people of Israel into Canaan, Jericho was the first city standing between them and the Promised Land. They had escaped Egypt by running through the Red Sea, which had parted miraculously for their passage, had wandered in the wilderness for forty years, had crossed the Jordan River, which had also parted for them, and now they had finally arrived at their divine destination only to hit a wall, literally—the defensive wall protecting the city of Jericho.

Despite God's promises, the Israelites were just as human as the rest of us and likely wondered how they could possibly conquer a fortified city like Jericho. Keep in mind that after Israel's escape from Egypt, Moses and Aaron had sent out twelve spies, including Joshua, for a reconnaissance of the land of Canaan. When they returned after forty 396370 days, ten of the spies thought they could never overtake the Canaanites, comparing themselves to grasshoppers in their midst (see Numbers 13:33). Only Joshua and Caleb had faith that the Lord would fulfill His promise and empower them to win this land.

As we might expect, then, fear and uncertainty swirled in the minds of the people of Israel upon encountering Jericho. Sure, God had come through for them time and time again, but how could they possibly defeat a walled city protected by an army?

Joshua may have questioned this himself because following their encampment, commemoration and rite of circumcision at Gilgal, he encountered an ominous stranger:

> Now when Joshua was near Jericho, he looked up and saw a man standing in front of him with a drawn sword in his hand. Joshua went up to him and asked, "Are you for us or for our enemies?"
>
> "Neither," he replied, "but as commander of the army of the LORD I have now come." Then Joshua fell facedown to the ground in reverence, and asked him, "What message does my Lord have for his servant?"
>
> The commander of the LORD's army replied, "Take off your sandals, for the place where you are standing is holy." And Joshua did so.
>
> Joshua 5:13–15

"Friend or foe?" Joshua basically asked this sword-wielding stranger, a question that demonstrated both wisdom and maturity. Instead of assuming, Joshua asked the man about his allegiance directly. As a leader, Joshua refused to jump to conclusions and to assume the worst, or the best, about this unknown loner. A good move, too, because as it turned out, the man's dramatic answer probably surprised him.

"I'm neither for you nor for your enemies, but here as commander of the Lord's army," the stranger replied. Wait a minute—

was the commander of the Lord's army saying he was not for the people of Israel? But God Himself had led them to this place as their new home. Why would this guy answer the way he did if he was really from God?

Perhaps the answer emerges from Joshua's reaction—he fell facedown and then removed his sandals because he was on holy ground. Joshua did not challenge this man's assertion and instruction but instead trusted that he was who he said he was, doing what God had sent him there to do.

I suspect this situation was a test God used to gauge the trust, humility and faith of His people. Entitlement and arrogance in Joshua's response would not honor God, nor would aggression and violence. Doubt and skepticism would be equally disrespectful. Instead, Joshua accepted the man at his word and engaged in the only response appropriate—worship. And just to be clear, he was not worshiping this man, who some scholars think was probably an angel; rather he was worshiping whom this man served—the one and only living and holy, almighty God.

In order to step into the promise of God, once again, we must remove every encumbrance even as we bow before Him. Any response other than worship makes it difficult to experience the fulfillment of His promises. When we surrender our hearts, minds, bodies and will before the Lord, we demonstrate complete reliance on His character, His power and His goodness. "Though he slay me, yet will I trust in him," Job declared in the midst of losing everything and everyone (Job 13:15 KJV).

Although Joshua did not face the same severity as Job in this particular test, the attitude of his heart was nonetheless under scrutiny. And he apparently passed with flying colors because God proceeded to instruct him how to conquer Jericho—with a promise that empowers us to persevere still today.

Risk Like Rahab

Joshua had learned from Moses that nothing is impossible with God. Whether parting seas and rivers or providing daily bread in the form of manna, the Lord always took care of His children's needs. Joshua knew that God wanted the people of Israel to claim the Promised Land. And Joshua also recognized that God was more powerful than any tribe, king, army or fortress. Looking up at the wall around Jericho, however, Joshua still had to wonder how it was going to come down.

Before I get ahead of our story, though, let me remind you that earlier, Joshua had ordered two of his men to spy out Jericho and note its defenses. His two lieutenants stayed at the home of Rahab, a prostitute who agreed to hide them from the king's men in exchange for the safety of her family when the Israelites attacked the city. She had heard of the Lord's power in rescuing the Israelites from Egypt and sustaining them in the desert until they reached Canaan (see Joshua 2).

Rahab's story by itself is an incredible example of trusting God, whom she knew very little about, to make a way forward where none existed. Logically, she had no reason to harbor the spies; she might have been putting at great risk the very family she wanted to save. But the Spirit of God must have gently whispered to her heart because she took a giant leap of faith. Not only did her bold step result in her family being spared, but she is named along with only three other women in Matthew's genealogy of Jesus (see Matthew 1:5).

In almost every mention of her, she is listed as Rahab the harlot or, depending on your translation, Rahab the prostitute. This sobriquet was not a spiteful condemnation but merely a way of identifying her by her vocation. If not in this line of work, she might have been known as Rahab the weaver or Rahab the baker.

Including her shameful profession each time she is mentioned, however, also reminds us, and basically everyone after Rahab's time, that God uses anyone willing to trust Him. Rahab was a Canaanite, automatically the enemy of the Israelites, as well as a prostitute, someone who earned a living by doing what the Lord had commanded the Israelites reserve exclusively for marriage between one man and one woman. Her great act of faith was to lie to her own countrymen, basically committing an act of treason.

Yet Rahab—arguably the least likely to serve God boldly, at least on paper—is also included in the "faith hall of fame" in Hebrews: "By faith the prostitute Rahab, because she welcomed the spies, was not killed with those who were disobedient" (Hebrews 11:31).

After the two spies left, she hung a red rope from a window in her house as a sign of her oath: She would not reveal the Israelites' intentions, and they would rescue her in the ensuing battle. Instead of wearing a scarlet letter branding her with shame and scorn—like Nathaniel Hawthorne's brave protagonist in his novel of a punishing Puritan society—Rahab used a crimson cord as a lifeline into her new identity.

By trusting God, Rahab experienced the fulfillment of a promise made to spare her life.

Her family lived because she risked everything on the God of those invading her city.

She discovered a new life beyond her wildest dreams—and a role in the ancestry of Jesus Christ.

Walls Came Tumblin' Down

Rahab seemed not to doubt that the Israelites, empowered and anointed by God, would bring down her city's walls, but I am not sure the people of Israel were quite so confident. Why? Because the Lord used Jericho to convey an important lesson to His people about finding their voice.

As we see here, they captured this ancient city located near the northwest tip of the Dead Sea, not by military might as much as sonic fright:

Now the gates of Jericho were securely barred because of the Israelites. No one went out and no one came in.

Then the LORD said to Joshua, "See, I have delivered Jericho into your hands, along with its king and its fighting men. March around the city once with all the armed men. Do this for six days. Have seven priests carry trumpets of rams' horns in front of the ark. On the seventh day, march around the city seven times, with the priests blowing the trumpets. When you hear them sound a long blast on the trumpets, have the whole army give a loud shout; then the wall of the city will collapse and the army will go up, everyone straight in."

Joshua 6:1–5

I love the way the Lord told Joshua that He had already delivered Jericho, including its king and army, into the Israelites' hands. Yes, *delivered*—past tense! God has already won our victories for us as well. Whatever your Jericho might be, the Lord has already delivered it into your hands, and now you must persevere to shout down its walls and claim His promise.

Maybe you are battling addiction to prescription medicines and you know you are not strong enough to win alone. Perhaps you are struggling to regain your health after the devastating impact of the pandemic. It could be your finances and the battle to get out of a debt that looms like the walls of Jericho in your life. You may be facing a conflict in your workplace, betrayal at home, rebellion from your children.

No matter what it is, the Lord has already won the battle for you—just as He won it for the people of Israel. Their part was to obey His instructions:

> On the seventh day, they got up at daybreak and marched around the city seven times in the same manner, except that on that day they circled the city seven times. The seventh time around, when the priests sounded the trumpet blast, Joshua commanded the army, "Shout! For the LORD has given you the city!"
>
> Joshua 6:15–16

Finding your voice and shouting out in obedience to the Lord remains a resounding theme from Jericho. In fact, you might know the song "Joshua Fit the Battle of Jericho"—perhaps you even learned it in Sunday school as a child. It is a well-known song believed to have its origin in the African American Gospel tradition of hymns composed and sung by slaves at the bittersweet dawn of our nation.

We can certainly understand why the Israelites' victory over Jericho appeals to an oppressed people praying for a day of liberation from powerful forces enslaving them—much like the Hebrews' prayers to be freed from the Egyptians before God empowered Moses to lead them home. The taking of Jericho is yet another classic underdog story. And while it inspires anyone facing seemingly insurmountable odds, the Jericho promise holds true for all of us.

What is the Jericho promise? It is the power of God to transform every wall we face into a bridge to a glorious future. It is the promise that the walls blocking your progress into the future

God has for you are about to come tumblin' down. It is the holy shout rumbling from your mouth until your throat is sore and your voice is hoarse. The Jericho promise is your expectation of God's power to make a way where you cannot—and the anticipation of what is waiting on the other side of your walls.

The Jericho promise is fundamental to your plow of perseverance and prophetic mantle of promotion. It is a holy shout-out to those who stand in your way that God is bringing them down. It is the heavenly trumpet blast celebrating the Jericho that God has already conquered in your life.

Walk, Worship, Win

It was no accident that Elijah, along with Elisha, went there on his farewell-to-earth tour because, like the other stops on his route, Jericho represents a timeless truth about who God is and how He loves us. If you want to see what you have never seen before, then you must claim the promises of God and believe in their ongoing fulfillment. You must persevere no matter how large the problem or how impossible the deficit.

In other words, do not be dismayed, baffled, perplexed or shaken when a wall appears in your journey.

Why?

Because, simply stated, there is a promise behind that wall.

There is an opportunity behind that obstacle.

There is God's favor behind your fear.

Wherever you are in your journey, the wall ahead cannot stop you.

That wall will become your bridge by the power of the living God.

The same Lord of heaven and earth who empowered the shouts of His people to bring down the walls of Jericho will empower you to do the same for the wall in your life. . . .

The wall of lack.

The wall of drama.

The wall of shame.

The wall of betrayal.

The wall of self-doubt.

The wall of disappointment.

The wall of anxiety.

The wall of fear.

The wall of failure.

The wall of deception.

The wall of illness and injury.

The wall of loneliness.

Keep in mind, however, that with every wall, we have choices. When we are faced with a wall, we have to depend on God even as we fulfill our part. We can go over the wall, we can go around the wall, or we can shout the wall down. If the decision were left to me, I would probably just climb over most walls I encounter. Or blast through them until I carved out a hole big enough to crawl through.

But it is not just about me—even as it is not just about you.

It is about the generations following in my footsteps, not only my children, and my children's children, and my children's children's children, but also the generations following after those who are looking to me—and to you—right now for leadership and encouragement, those we walk alongside as we help bring down their walls. It is about the Elishas whom you will mentor, the apprentices you will find in the field plowing before draping your mantle of promotion and prophetic power over them.

We have, therefore, only one viable option: We must shout down the walls that bind us.

Because I do not want those who follow after me to have to face what I am facing today.

Just as you do not want those who follow after you to endure what you have battled for so long.

If we want our walls to become their bridges, then we must shout those walls down.

We must shout down the walls separating us from where we are and where God wants us to be. We must shout down the adversaries and the obstacles blocking our paths. We must obliterate our walls so that those whom we encourage and mentor and nurture—and those who come after them—will climb over the rubble and give God thanks and praise for what He did through us. They will read the plaques and get tears in their eyes, recognizing and celebrating the fact that someone loved them enough to bring down these walls so that they would not be incarcerated by them.

They will have their own walls to bring down, but they will not have to deal with the walls God allowed you and me to shout into crumbled ruins. When we live in the Jericho promise of God's power to persevere, we keep marching until it is time to shout. And then we *shout*—both with our voice and the posture of our soul—as if we mean it! Raising our volume and deepening our faith, we speak truth with conviction, we drown the voice of the enemy in our praises of God, and we declare God's promises to us. When you confront a trial, a temptation, a trauma or a tempest, then you know what to do.

You must be willing by faith in Jesus Christ to go around it, praise it down with your shouts, and then climb over it. You march, then you praise, then you climb. You walk, you worship—and you win.

Shouts Echo

Elijah took Elisha to Jericho as a reminder to use his voice as an instrument of the Lord. To shout down his fears and overcome those who would stand in the way of the work Elisha was inheriting. Remember what Elisha told the group of prophets who asked him if he knew that God was about to take Elijah to heaven that very day? "Yes, I know, so be quiet." His reply might strike us as disrespectful, but if we assume that is not the case, then for what other reason would he silence these spectators?

Telling them to be quiet contrasts with God's directive to Joshua and the Israelites to shout in Jericho. But think about this for a moment. This group of prophets was telling something Elisha already knew, which they probably knew he already knew! They were wasting their breath, literally, because they wanted to demonstrate that they, too, were God's chosen. They were insiders and based their identity not on serving God, but on how serving Him could elevate their status with others.

When we speak to elevate ourselves, the result often backfires. We come across either as arrogant, cocky and overly confident, or as incredibly boastful, foolish and out of touch with reality. Rather than wait until God instructs us to speak, we talk to impress others and make ourselves look better. Without humility and dependence on God, the Jericho promise is merely a whisper and not a shout. Remember, whispers fade while shouts echo.

Rather than be part of a group that shows off its insider's knowledge, surround yourself with people who will not grow weary from the march. People willing to work in unison for a higher purpose and a heavenly goal. People willing to shout all at once.

If it is not time to shout, then we would be wise to heed Elisha's instruction and keep quiet. God does not give us wisdom or provide guidance so that we can impress others or showcase our elite status as His prophets. Remember that before He told Joshua what to do in order to bring down Jericho, God sent the commander of His army to meet him. I cannot help but wonder if the Lord's directive would have been different, or taken longer to execute, if Joshua had not displayed humility and reverence on holy ground.

Before we march into battle and prepare to shout, we must spend time worshiping God. Holy ground comes before the battleground. If we expect to experience the Jericho promise and see our walls tumble, then we must be immersed in God's Spirit and God's Word. Our eyes must be fixed on God's Son. Focus on the holy before you holler!

The Jordan Discovery

Elijah and Elisha could hear the echoes of those shouts from Joshua and the Israelites so many generations later, if not audibly then spiritually. And their visit there must have been bittersweet, because after Jericho there remained but one final destination before the Lord swept Elijah up to heaven: Jordan. After they repeated their script of "Stay here!" and "I will never leave you," the two prophets reached the riverbank, along with fifty peers once again spectating.

Now if it strikes you as odd that Elijah and Elisha had these people following behind them, then consider that Elijah's followers fell into one of two groups. On the one hand, Elisha walked alongside him and learned from him. As we have seen, Elisha refused to stay put despite his mentor's directive. He was committed to God and to Elijah in a way that would not allow him to leave his teacher's side.

In contrast to this kind of personal devotion, Elijah had others who followed him only to watch at a distance. They were not there to learn from him or serve God alongside him. They just wanted to enjoy the show. To tell others what was going to happen next. To say they had seen the amazing prophet of God who defeated the prophets of Baal.

Whether you consider yourself a prophet or not, you will encounter the same two types of people.

There are those who will be right next to you, walking alongside you.

And then there are those who will watch you from a distance.

The distance people are those who will keep an eye on you to see if you still have it.

The distance people are those who will be watching you to see if the anointing still works.

The distance people will follow you with the unfortunate anticipation of seeing you fall or fail.

Do not be defined by the distance people.

Do not be defined by the people who think they know you, when they do not know you at all! Basically, when it comes to distance people, what they think and what they say and what they post has zero value.

If they have not prayed with me, then their perspective does not matter.

If they have not walked with me, then their wisdom does not matter.

If they have not fought with me, then their following does not matter.

If you want power to persevere in your life, then surround yourself with people who speak "into" you and not about you.

Surround yourself with people who speak about your future and not about your past.

Surround yourself with people who say, "Look what the Lord has done!" and not "Look what the devil can do!"

If you are looking for a description of this kind of person, then you cannot do better than Psalm 1:

> Blessed is the one who does not walk in step with the wicked or stand in the way that sinners take or sit in the company of mockers, but whose delight is in the law of the LORD, and who meditates on his law day and night. That person is like a tree planted by streams of water, which yields its fruit in season and whose leaf does not wither—whatever they do prospers.
>
> Not so the wicked! They are like chaff that the wind blows away. Therefore the wicked will not stand in the judgment, nor sinners in the assembly of the righteous.
>
> For the LORD watches over the way of the righteous, but the way of the wicked leads to destruction.
>
> Psalm 1:1–6

These are the people who will go the distance with you, marching, shouting and refusing to stay behind when God calls you on. These are the people you want in your life, both on the journey and when you reach the next place—whether you are leveling Jericho or preparing to cross the Jordan.

The Way and the Waymaker

When the two prophets reached the impasse of the flowing river, Elijah used his Jericho promise to make a Jordan discovery. Having lived a lifetime of watching God do the impossible, Elijah likely was not fazed by the issue of how to cross the river. Perhaps with little fanfare despite those watching from a distance, the prophet did what came naturally by this time in his life—*super*naturally: "Elijah took his cloak, rolled it up and struck the water with it. The water divided to the right and to the left, and the two of them crossed over on dry ground" (2 Kings 2:8).

The cloak represented divine authority.

The cloak represented the calling.

The cloak represented the anointing.

The cloak represented the gift.

Elijah did not tell Elisha the cloak works.

Elijah did not tell Elisha prayer works. Elijah did not tell Elisha that holy living works.

Elijah did not tell Elisha obeying the word of God works.

Elijah did not tell Elisha to go to the Jordan and see if the mantle works.

Elijah demonstrated.

Elijah showed Elisha what to do, when to do it and how it got done.

He communicated this to him silently: "Okay, son, I'm going to show you what to do whenever you find yourself in front of a circumstance where there is no way to get across. I'm not going to tell you how to do it, but I'm going to show you. You take the anointing, the authority, the gift, the grace that God has given you and exercise it. You look at the obstacle, take what you have, place what you have on what's in front of you, and God guarantees that He will make a way where there is no way. Watch carefully because I'm not going to tell you—I'm going to show you."

We need a generation of leaders who will show the emerging generation how to do it! People who say, "I'm not going to tell you how to live in victory; I'm going to show you what it is to live in victory. I'm not just going to tell you how to overcome; I'm going to show you how to overcome." They communicate *Watch me!* without having to say a word.

Watch me move that mountain.

Watch me kick that devil out.

Watch me demand that that infirmity shrivel up.

Watch me shout down walls.

Watch me pray down the fire.

Watch me slay that giant.

Watch me come out of the furnace—with a tan!

Watch me come out of that storm with a brand-new ship.

Watch me tell the fox that I will continue to preach the Word and heal the sick.

Watch me shift my atmosphere.

Before Elijah departed, he left his heir the greatest gift he had to give. He showed him one powerful truth: *Our God is the Waymaker.*

We must live in the power of the Jordan discovery just as Elisha did.

God will make a way where there is no way.

He will make a way when all the doors close in your face.

He will make a way when your detractors say, "No way."

He will make a way when hell says, "No *way!*"

He will make a way when you say, "No *way!*"

God's Word distills the essence of what Elijah showed Elisha at the Jordan River that day:

"I am the Lord, your Holy One, Israel's Creator and King. I am the Lord, who opened a way through the waters, making a dry path through the sea. . . .

"But forget all that—it is nothing compared to what I am going to do. For I am about to do something new. See, I have already begun! Do you not see it? I will make a pathway through the wilderness. I will create rivers in the dry wasteland."

Isaiah 43:15–16, 18–19 NLT

Keep in mind: God is not just the Waymaker.

Jesus tells us that He is the Way (see John 14:6).

When you are in Christ and He is in you, there will always be a way.

He is the way out of bondage, out of failure, out of sin, out of defeat.

He is the way through the storm, through the trial, through the test.

And He is the way into abundant life, eternal life, new life, favored life, glorious life and victorious life.

If you want the power to persevere to promotion, then follow the Waymaker.

He leveled Jericho's walls and parted Jordan's waters.

There is nothing He cannot do for you!

Push Your Plow, Meet Your Mantle

Sometimes we struggle to walk by faith because we grow impatient waiting for God to fulfill His promises to us in the ways we expect. As we have seen, He is often waiting for us to mature. But His promises are real and timeless, and He is the same yesterday, today and tomorrow. In order to experience the kind of prophetic power that sustains your journey of faith, you must march, worship and watch your walls come down. When you reach the next river without a bridge, you know what to do. Use your cloak and trust God to keep you dry as you walk across the water!

1. When have you experienced the fulfillment of a promise from God? How long had you been waiting? What did you learn from the experience?

2. What Jericho is currently looming ahead of you, blocking your path and demanding to be conquered before you can proceed? What are the walls you must shout down in order to receive what God has already delivered?

3. When was the last time you made a Jordan discovery and learned by watching another believer trust God's power to accomplish something supernaturally? When was the last time you practiced this yourself?

Dear Waymaker, there are so many times when I do not see how I can go on, when the walls of my Jericho seem too tall and impenetrable. But even as I choose to trust You and obey You, I also choose to march, worship and shout down those walls. I pray for the kind of faith that I see in Elijah and Elisha, the kind Joshua had as he led the people of Israel around the city walls of Jericho. I know that every time I hit a wall, You have already made a way for me! I give You all my thanks and praise, Lord. All the glory is Yours and Yours alone. Amen.

10

Your Double Portion

Never become so enamored of what you carry that you forget who carries you—the God of the mantle is much more important than the mantle of God!

I recently celebrated the golden anniversary of my birth—in other words, I turned fifty! While many people consider this age to be the tipping point of middle age, I made it clear to my friends and family that if they really loved me, then there would be no "over the hill" banners, black balloons or funereal jokes at my birthday party. Instead, I wanted to savor and celebrate the many amazing milestones of God's goodness in my life.

Entering this new decade of my life, I confess that I do not run as fast as I used to run most days. But I like to think I am a smarter runner who knows when and how to push beyond my limitations to attempt a new personal best. I might not have the energy and stamina to go nights without sleep while pouring myself into a new ministry, new book or new movie. But I like to believe I have learned to appreciate the value of a Sabbath rest in order to recharge my body, mind and spirit. I might not schedule as many meetings, appointments and conferences as when I was a younger man. But I know without a doubt that I am more productive for what matters most—investing my life for eternal purposes.

I no longer get frantic and stressed—okay, *as* frantic and stressed—when unexpected events derail my plans and postpone my goals. I have now been forced to rely on God's timing, provision and guidance more than enough to trust that He knows best. Nevertheless, I still feel pressure to accomplish all the things I am called to do in order to advance His heavenly Kingdom here on earth.

On those days when I am overwhelmed by all I hope to accomplish, I often pray the psalmist's prayer:

"Show me, LORD, my life's end and the number of my days; let me know how fleeting my life is. You have made my days a mere handbreadth; the span of my years is as nothing before you. Everyone is but a breath, even those who seem secure."

Psalm 39:4–5

Ironically, remembering that my days are numbered takes the pressure off! I realize that I need to focus only on what the Lord calls me to do this day. Rather than make me shortsighted, surrendering my will to His on a daily basis provides an eternal perspective.

Maximize Your Mantle

Recent birthdays are not the only factor reminding me to make the most of my time. As a pastor I also see the tragic loss when someone's death leaves unfinished business for his or her loved ones here on earth. There is nothing sadder than preaching the funeral of someone who left loving words unspoken and faithful deeds undone. Someone whose life was spent focused more on the urgent and temporary than the essential and eternal.

We can never know for sure what tomorrow holds. We think we know what to expect. We assume we can control our schedules, our plans, our comings and goings, both today and in years to come. But our lives are not within our power to control; nor do we know how long we will have here: "Teach us to realize the brevity of life, so that we may grow in wisdom" (Psalm 90:12 NLT).

As we conclude our journey with Elijah and Elisha in these pages, it seems appropriate to focus on making the most of what we have been given during our time on earth, to maximize our mantles through the power of the Holy Spirit to persevere. This focus helps us keep our eyes on the prize and ensures that we create an eternal legacy worthy of the One we serve.

So many people lose their momentum and get distracted from what is truly important. Many know they spend too much time at work or in pursuit of pleasure, but they put off aligning their behavior with their priorities until it is too late. They know they need to ask for forgiveness for how they have hurt others in their lives, often the ones they love the most. And they are aware they also need to forgive those who have hurt them.

But knowing the truth of the matter and acting on what we know are both crucially, and often cruelly, distinct: "You do not know what your life will be like tomorrow. For you are just a vapor that appears for a little while and then vanishes away" (James 4:14 NASB).

Perhaps there is no greater regret than leaving things half done instead of leaving others a double portion.

When Bigger Is Not Better

When you consider inheritance, it is tempting to think in concrete terms and assume that more is better. Many people accumulate wealth but rarely enjoy it themselves, focused instead on leaving their precious possessions, numerous investments and multizillion-dollar bank accounts to future generations. They strive but never enjoy the fruit of their labors, let alone invest it in an eternal legacy. Even those of more modest means plan ahead so that they can make life easier for the coming generations—at least that is the assumption.

But inheriting money and valuable resources does not necessarily make anyone's life easier. According to God's Word, sometimes the more you have, the more you want:

> Those who want to get rich fall into temptation and a trap and into many foolish and harmful desires that plunge people into ruin and destruction. For the love of money is a root of all kinds of evil. Some people, eager for money, have wandered from the faith and pierced themselves with many griefs.
>
> 1 Timothy 6:9–10

When someone dies without leaving a will, and even sometimes when leaving a will, the legal battle over the estate can be both fierce and messy among the heirs. The prospect of inheriting money motivates many people to say and do things for their own benefit without regard for anyone else. And the size of the estate or amount of the inheritance does not have to be very much for people to fight over it. I have witnessed many families torn apart over who got Grandma's china cabinet or Dad's coin collection. I recall one family being divided because they all wanted their mother's Holy Bible!

During His time on earth, Jesus encountered a situation where He was asked to intervene in the matter of awarding an inheritance:

Someone in the crowd said to him, "Teacher, tell my brother to divide the inheritance with me."

Jesus replied, "Man, who appointed me a judge or an arbiter between you?" Then he said to them, "Watch out! Be on your guard against all kinds of greed; life does not consist in an abundance of possessions."

And he told them this parable: "The ground of a certain rich man yielded an abundant harvest. He thought to himself, 'What shall I do? I have no place to store my crops.'

"Then he said, 'This is what I'll do. I will tear down my barns and build bigger ones, and there I will store my surplus grain. And I'll say to myself, "You have plenty of grain laid up for many years. Take life easy; eat, drink and be merry."'

"But God said to him, 'You fool! This very night your life will be demanded from you. Then who will get what you have prepared for yourself?'

"This is how it will be with whoever stores up things for themselves but is not rich toward God."

Luke 12:13–21

Let me tell you, I think of that parable almost every time I drive past a storage facility. In our country many of us have more than enough, and yet we rent temperature-controlled concrete caverns where we can store the items we have no room for at home—including the furniture, tchotchkes, trinkets and would-be treasures we inherited from our parents and grandparents. Jesus made it unequivocally clear in His response here that bigger is not better when it comes to material possessions and wealth. He also provided the reason for this truth: "Where your treasure is, there your heart will be also" (Luke 12:34).

This parable reminds us to focus on creating a legacy that will transcend anything here on earth "where moths and vermin destroy, and where thieves break in and steal" (Matthew 6:19). Instead, we should use our time, treasure and talent to "store up for yourselves treasures in heaven, where moths and vermin do not destroy, and where thieves do not break in and steal" (Matthew 6:20).

If you want to make your life count for eternity, then the kind of inheritance you value most should also be the kind you leave behind. The same kind that Elisha requested from Elijah.

Double Trouble

After they had crossed the Jordan River, thanks to God's power focused in Elijah's miraculous mantle, it was time to say good-bye. They had now traveled to Gilgal, Bethel and Jericho, each stop a commemorative place of worship and wonder for what it represented in both their national and personal history. There, on the other side of the Jordan, not only did Elijah want to leave his apprentice with a legacy, but apparently he also wanted to fulfill Elisha's expectations for what that legacy might be.

"Tell me, what can I do for you before I am taken from you?" Elijah offered. We have no idea how time passed between his question and Elisha's reply: "Let me inherit a double portion of your spirit" (2 Kings 2:9). Whether this answer was something he had thoughtfully pondered many times or an immediate awareness in that moment, we are not told.

Either way, however, Elisha's audacious request is not one many heirs utter to their benefactors. He did not simply ask for an inheritance. He did not merely request a spiritual blessing. Elisha wanted a double portion of the spirit, the power, the authority and the anointing he had witnessed in Elijah. The heir to the role of God's prophet dared to ask for everything he knew his mentor possessed—times two!

You see, the power to persevere is not for those who are satisfied with a normal standard portion. This mantle is for those who will not settle for anything less than double, triple and more—direct access to the infinite, unlimited power of the living God! The stronger your faith, the more spiritual power you can facilitate as a conduit of God's grace, blessings and miracles. The fact that Elisha asked for a double portion indicates not only that he believed it possible but also that he could handle it.

Indeed, his teacher recognized the enormity of the request: "'You have asked a difficult thing,' Elijah said, 'yet if you see me when I am taken from you, it will be yours—otherwise, it will not'" (2 Kings 2:10). In giving his answer, Elijah seems aware of two truths. First, no matter how willing he was to bless Elisha in this way, ultimately it was up to the Lord. Nonetheless, in his wisdom Elijah provided Elisha with a confirmation signal.

In addition, Elijah had just gone through the most difficult chapters of his life. If that was his "single portion," which he found challenging to endure, then was Elisha actually ready for twice as much? I can just hear him saying, "Are you kidding, son? You know the difficult time I had carrying a single portion, and now you're saying you want twice what I've been carrying? Twice as much sorrow over Israel's rebellion and idolatry? Twice as much calamity from droughts, holy fire and rainstorms? Twice as much danger at the hands of wicked leaders like Ahab and Jezebel?"

Elisha probably knew he was asking for double trouble.

But he also knew he was asking for double the divine presence of God's Spirit!

Grasp the Great

Now, if I had been in either of their sandals, Elijah's or Elisha's, I would have been eager to discuss this imminent spiritual inheritance. If I were Elijah, I would want to give as much advice, counsel, recommendations and parting words of blessing as possible. If I were Elisha, I would be filled with questions about experiencing God, listening to His Spirit, and following the Lord through trials and tempests.

Perhaps they had such a conversation because we are told they continued "walking along and talking together" (2 Kings 2:11), but we are not given the details. What we are told, however, is that Elijah's transportation for transformation finally arrived:

> As they were walking along and talking together, suddenly a chariot of fire and horses of fire appeared and separated the two of them, and Elijah went up to heaven in a whirlwind. Elisha saw this and cried out, "My father! My father! The chariots and horsemen of Israel!" And Elisha saw him no more. Then he took hold of his garment and tore it in two.
>
> Elisha then picked up Elijah's cloak that had fallen from him and went back and stood on the bank of the Jordan. He took the cloak that had fallen from Elijah and struck the water with it. "Where now is the LORD, the God of Elijah?" he asked. When he struck the water, it divided to the right and to the left, and he crossed over.
>
> 2 Kings 2:11–13

Talk about a dramatic exit! Other than the Ascension of our Savior, Jesus, Himself, I cannot think of a more incredible description in Scripture of passing from earth to heaven. To my knowledge, there is only one other disclosure in the Bible about

Mantle 2.0 that Elisha received, his request for a double-portion upgrade was fulfilled.

Returning to the riverbank where the two of them had stood only a short time before, Elisha wasted no time in seeking God's presence. Elisha did what he had just seen Elijah do and struck the water with the inherited cloak, asking, "Where now is the LORD, the God of Elijah?" (2 Kings 2:14). Remember how Elijah taught Elisha by doing rather than just telling him what to do? We see in that moment that his efforts produced fruit.

Also, notice in the process that Elisha did not ask "Where is Elijah?" but "Where is the Lord?" While he probably already missed his teacher, Elisha knew where Elijah was—in heaven—and knew he no longer needed help in answering God's call on his life. Instead, Elisha was keenly aware that he needed to connect immediately with the power source of his predecessor, the God of Elijah. The Lord answered Elisha's question miraculously by displaying the same result Elijah had received earlier: The river divided, and Elisha went across (see 2 Kings 2:14).

I wonder if Elisha was thinking, *If He did it for him, He will do it for me!* Perhaps he could not wait to see if the mantle he had inherited was the real deal. And it is interesting for us to consider which possibility frightened him more—that he would actually get what he had requested, or that he would have to deal with the disappointment that his prophetic increase was not happening just yet after all.

Sometimes when God gives us what we ask for, we seem as surprised as anyone else! Some people, I suspect, never receive the next mantle of promotion because they fail even to ask for it. The disappointment of asking and not receiving eclipses their desire for more. So they settle for the mantle they have rather than risk it for the double portion God wants to give them.

Once again, we must be willing to leave one mantle behind in order to pick up the next one. As Jesus explained to His followers, communication with our heavenly Father and faith in His goodness are the keys:

"Ask and it will be given to you; seek and you will find; knock and the door will be opened to you. For everyone who asks receives; the one who seeks finds; and to the one who knocks, the door will be opened.

"Which of you, if your son asks for bread, will give him a stone? Or if he asks for a fish, will give him a snake? If you, then, though you are evil, know how to give good gifts to your children, how much more will your Father in heaven give good gifts to those who ask him! So in everything, do to others what you would have them do to you, for this sums up the Law and the Prophets."

Matthew 7:7–12

Consider His final point here: the correlation between getting what we request from a good and loving Father and treating other people as we ourselves long to be treated. In other words, our motives for making particular requests matter. If we are asking only for what is good for us, then we are missing the opportunity to be a conduit of blessing for others. When we are focused only on our own gain, then, ironically, we lose our double portion. When we get impatient and try to sew our mantle together instead of waiting on God's timing for the next one He has for us, then we should not wonder why our homemade garment lacks spiritual power.

Notice, too, that Jesus said *in everything* do to others what you would have them do to you. Jesus did not say practice this occasionally or sometimes or when you are in a jam or when you have nowhere else to turn. He did not say treat others as you want to be treated when it is convenient or comfortable, politically correct or expedient. No. He said *in everything* we must reflect this Golden Rule!

How can we expect God to give us everything we ask for, especially His power, if we intend to use it for ourselves and not His Kingdom? For our comfort and not the needs of others? For our own elevation and not the elevation of the cross? Simply put, we cannot. If we want to claim the inheritance we have in Christ so that we can leave others an even greater portion, then we must practice more than we preach.

We must walk more than we talk.

We must show more than we tell.

We must act more than we wish.

We must move more than we stand still.

We must have the kind of faith that provides the power to persevere.

Your Kind of Faith

Just as Elisha learned how to rely on God from Elijah, we must also build an inheritance that shows others how to carry on our spiritual legacy. In other words, someday those who come after you will look back and believe that if it worked for you, then it will work for them. God has entrusted you with His riches in Christ so that you can share His love, reflect His grace, reveal His mercy and give to others as He has given to you. This is the legacy we have received and will someday leave behind, "so that being justified by his grace we might become heirs according to the hope of eternal life" (Titus 3:7 ESV).

But know as well that God expects you to invest the legacy you received in order for it to grow. Like the servants in the parable

Jesus told about the master entrusting them with his wealth, you must not bury your talents in the ground. You must never allow fear to guide you but rather the bold faith of God's Spirit within you. His power in you allows you to put personal security and comfort aside in order to sacrifice and serve. God's Word tells us,

> In him we have obtained an inheritance, having been predestined according to the purpose of him who works all things according to the counsel of his will, so that we who were the first to hope in Christ might be to the praise of his glory.
>
> Ephesians 1:11–12

The spiritual legacy you inherited must be invested so that those who follow you can experience an even greater portion—yes, a double portion—of God's power overflowing in their lives. You must focus on the big picture, an eternal perspective, rather than just your lifetime or even that of the next generation. You want to look ahead and think about the impact you can have on all generations who come after you to ensure maximum impact. "A good man leaves an inheritance to his children's children," the Bible says, "but the sinner's wealth is laid up for the righteous" (Proverbs 13:22 esv). If we fail to use our mantles for God's purposes, then we will lose them so that others can!

For us today, our mantles are made of wood—the cross of Christ. Jesus made it clear: "If any of you wants to be my follower, you must give up your own way, take up your cross daily, and follow me" (Luke 9:23 NLT). This is the path to spiritual riches and eternal treasures in heaven, but it is also the power source for our needs and provisions right now. When we let go of the mantles that we believe elevate and define us, we discover a deeper, stronger, richer faith.

This is the kind of faith required to part rivers and call down fire from heaven. This is the kind of faith necessary to leave a double portion of spiritual power for future generations. This is the kind of faith that makes a way now so that others who follow see how it is done. This is the kind of faith that celebrates the Gilgal of arrival, commemorates the dream given at Bethel, shouts down the walls of Jericho, and parts the Jordan with power so that we can walk forward into that which God has already provided for us!

This is the kind of double-portion, Trinity-loving, singular-focused faith that uses God's power to turn walls into bridges. The kind that makes it clear nothing will be the same.

The kind that declares

Addiction dies in my generation.

Alcoholism dies in my generation.

Adultery dies in my generation.

Sexual promiscuity dies in my generation.

Hatred dies in my generation.

Poverty dies in my generation.

Diabetes, cancer and heart disease end in my generation.

Suicide dies in my generation.

Divorce dies in my generation.

Depression, anxiety and fear end in my generation.

Goliath will fall in my generation.

Delilah will be stopped in my generation.

And the glory will not be stolen in my generation.

This ends right here, right now, in Jesus' name!

This kind of faith builds an inheritance that will move mountains now and part seas later. The kind others will recall as a source of strength, inspiration and motivation. "Let each generation tell its children of your mighty acts; let them proclaim your power" (Psalm 145:4 NLT). This kind of Jesus-loving power hears the sounds clamoring within the walls binding our broken world today.

The sound of desperation.

The sound of a nation torn apart by the devil of discord.

The sound of those desperately hurting and in need of healing.

But those with a double portion of spiritual power also hear those walls coming down.

They hear the sound of their shouts transforming walls into bridges.

They hear the sound of black, white, brown and yellow coming together.

They hear the sound of pastors, worshipers, intercessors, prayer warriors coming together.

The sound of one Church bringing down the Goliath of hatred with the stone of love.

The sound of one Church confronting the Herod of bigotry with the sword of the Spirit.

The sound of one Church telling the pharaohs of the 21st century, "Let my people go so they may worship!"

The sound of one Church that will remind all of humanity that our hands are made to create, our mouths are made to speak truth with love, our hearts are made to forgive and our knees are meant for prayer.

The sound of one Church that will not be controlled by politics but will worship only the Lamb who is the Lion of the tribe of Judah.

The sound of one Church coming together that will not water down the Gospel, that will speak truth with love, that will preach the Word in and out of season, fulfill the Great Commission, make disciples, equip the saints, worship God in spirit and in truth, bring the Good News to the poor, freedom to the captives, healing to the brokenhearted, and that will declare this to be the year of the Lord's favor. One Church with all members seeking justice, loving mercy and walking humbly before God.

The sound of a Father-glorifying, Christ-exalting, Spirit-empowered, mountain-moving, devil-rebuking, demon-binding, atmosphere-shifting, world-changing, holy, healed, healthy, happy, humble, hungry, honoring Church!

The sound of your own voice claiming the double portion that you inherited through the blood of Jesus Christ on the cross. The sound of your own voice claiming the spiritual inheritance that breaks down every barrier and overcomes every enemy.

Can you hear your voice? I dare you to open your mouth and declare:

My heart is healed.
My mind is sound.
My soul is blessed.
My family is chosen.
My body is healthy.
My future is fantastic.
My words are anointed.
My walk is righteous.
My praise is dangerous.
My destiny is unstoppable.
My life is Emmanuel.
My all is Christ!

Rightfully Yours

If you want to experience the power to persevere in your life, then it is time to move from your plow to your mantle and from your mantle to your double portion.

It is time to live as a co-heir with Christ instead of a distant relative ashamed to show up in God's House.

It is time to stop trying on your own and start dying to self.

It is time to seek God's power and exercise your mantle.

It is time to survive the drought, overcome the idols, call down the fire, soak in the rain, tuck and run the race of faith, keep your eyes on the prize and live in the abundance of your double portion.

It is time to start living in the fullness of the power of God's Spirit dwelling in you. With the apostle Paul, we can declare:

God's Spirit makes us sure that we are his children. His Spirit lets us know that together with Christ we will be given what God has promised. We will also share in the glory of Christ, because we have suffered with him. I am sure that what we are suffering now cannot compare with the glory that will be shown to us.

Romans 8:16–18 CEV

Your divine double portion means you experience contentment now and fulfillment later. Your spiritual inheritance means that your debt to sin has been paid. Your suffering means you share in Christ's glory.

It is time to claim what is rightfully yours and surrender what is no longer your concern.

Do not claim ownership over the curse.

Claim ownership over the blessings.

Do not claim ownership of the problem.

Claim ownership of the promises.

If it is not holy, you do not want it.

If it is not blessed, you do not need it.

If it is not going to give God all of the glory, you must not desire any part of it.

Instead, live in the fullness of faith, fellowship and friendship as you claim what is yours in Christ. . . .

What is yours is righteousness (see 2 Corinthians 5:21).

What is yours is peace (see Philippians 1:2).

What is yours is joy (see John 15:11).

What is yours is eternal life (see John 3:16).

What is yours is new life (see 2 Corinthians 5:17).

What is yours is abundant life (see John 10:10).

What is yours is a destiny that cannot be stopped, a dream that cannot be quenched and a designation that cannot be undone.

You are saved by grace.

You have the power to persevere!

Push Your Plow, Meet Your Mantle

As our journey with Elijah and Elisha comes to a close, use the following questions to help you review and reflect on the thoughts and feelings you have experienced while reading this book. Think about where you were spiritually when you began and the progress you have made since then. Finally, spend some time alone with God in prayer, asking Him for the power to persevere as you serve Him and others with your current mantle of promotion. Give Him thanks and praise as you move forward in the full power of the Holy Spirit, confident that He who started this good work in you will be faithful to complete it.

1. What idea, theme or spiritual truth stands out to you from this book? How does this takeaway emerge in the lives of Elijah and Elisha? Consider what incident from their journey together has the greatest impact on you or stands out the most.

2. When has God led you to relinquish one mantle in order to pick up the next mantle of promotion in your life? What three words would you use to describe this process of transition or season of change? Why?

3. As you consider your spiritual legacy, what needs to change in your life so you can invest more time, attention and resources in the eternal inheritance you want to leave for future generations? What will be the "double portion" you leave those who come after you?

Dear God of the Mantle, You have brought me so far on my journey of faith. Thank You, Lord, for the way You always sustain me with Your power and guide me through each trial and triumph I encounter, whether I am pushing my plow or wearing Your mantle. As I seek to serve You with the faithfulness of Elijah and Elisha, I ask that Your will be done in my life. I want to honor and glorify only You and not myself. I will trust You and Your timing as I seek the double portion You have for me—more of Your love, Your power, Your provision, Your joy, Your peace and Your purpose. I am so grateful for all You have taught me and shown me through these pages. Amen.

Samuel Rodriguez is president of the National Hispanic Christian Leadership Conference (NHCLC), the world's largest Hispanic Christian organization, with more than 42,000 U.S. churches and many additional churches spread throughout the Spanish-speaking diaspora.

Rodriguez stands recognized by CNN, FOX News, Univision and Telemundo as America's most influential Latino/Hispanic faith leader. *Charisma* magazine named him one of the forty leaders who changed the world. *The Wall Street Journal* named him one of the top twelve Latino leaders, and he was the only faith leader on that list. He has been named among the "Top 100 Christian Leaders in America" (*Newsmax* 2018) and nominated as one of the "100 Most Influential People in the World" (*Time* 2013). Rodriguez is regularly featured on CNN, Fox News, Univision, PBS, *Christianity Today*, *The New York Times*, *The Wall Street Journal* and many others.

Rodriguez was the first Latino to deliver the keynote address at the annual Martin Luther King Jr. Commemorative Service at Ebenezer Baptist Church, and is a recipient of the Martin Luther King Jr. Leadership Award presented by the Congress of Racial Equality.

Rodriguez advised former American presidents Bush, Obama and Trump, and frequently consults with Congress advancing immigration and criminal justice reform as well as religious freedom and pro-life initiatives. By the grace of God, the Rev. Samuel Rodriguez is one of the few individuals to have participated in the inauguration ceremonies of two different presidents, representing both political parties.

In January 2009, Pastor Sam read from the gospel of Luke for President Obama's inaugural morning service at Saint John's

Episcopal Church. On January 20, 2017, at Mr. Trump's inauguration, with more than one billion people watching from around the world, Pastor Sam became the first Latino Evangelical to participate in a U.S. presidential inaugural ceremony, reading from Matthew 5 and concluding with "In Jesus' name!" In April 2020, Rev. Rodriguez was appointed to the National Coronavirus Recovery Commission to offer specialized experience and expertise in crisis mitigation and recovery to help national, state and local leaders guide America through the COVID-19 pandemic.

Rodriguez is executive producer of two films: *Breakthrough*, the GMA Dove Award–winner for Inspirational Film of the Year, with also an Academy Award nomination for Best Original Song; and *Flamin' Hot*, in partnership with Franklin Entertainment and 20th Century Fox. He is also co-founder of TBN Salsa, an international Christian-based broadcast television network, and he is the author of *You Are Next, Shake Free, Be Light* (a #1 *Los Angeles Times* bestseller), and *From Survive to Thrive*, a #1 Amazon bestseller.

He earned his master's degree from Lehigh University and received honorary doctorates from Northwest, William Jessup and Baptist University of the Americas.

Rodriguez serves as Senior Pastor of New Season Church, one of America's fastest growing mega-churches and #13 on *Newsmax*'s "Top 50" mega-churches in America, with campuses in Los Angeles and Sacramento, California, where he resides with his wife, Eva, and their three children.

For more information, please visit
www.PastorSam.com
Rev. Samuel Rodriguez
@pastorsamuelrodriguez
@nhclc

Spanish Edition of *Persevere with Power* Also Available

Inspirado en la historia de la fidelidad de Eliseo, el exitoso autor Samuel Rodriguez explora el poder de perseverar con esperanza en medio de los tiempos oscuros en los que vivimos. Si las luchas interminables te han dejado cansado y desanimado, entonces entérate que es posible no solo liberarte sino también descubrir la asignación, la unción y la autoridad que Dios tiene preparadas para ti.

Persevera con poder